NINJA WOO[DFIRE]

OUTDOOR GRILL

& SMOKER COOKBOOK

Simple & Mouth-Watering Recipes for Ninja Woodfire Electric Pellet | Your Expert Guide to BBQ, Grilling, Bake, Roast, Dehydrate, and Broil

Jerry Haslett

Table Of Content

CHAPTER 8: POULTRY 57

CHAPTER 9: SNACK AND DESSERT 65

APPENDIX 1: BASIC KITCHEN CONVERSIONS & EQUIVALENTS 73

APPENDIX 2: NINJA WOODFIRE OUTDOOR GRILL TIMETABLE..........74

APPENDIX 3: RECIPES INDEX 78

Introduction

Ignite your culinary creativity and embark on a mouthwatering journey with the Ninja Woodfire Outdoor Grill & Smoker Recipes Cookbook! Within these pages, you'll discover a treasure trove of irresistible recipes specially crafted to showcase the incredible capabilities of your Ninja Woodfire Outdoor Grill & Smoker. From juicy steaks perfectly seared over an open flame to tender, slow-smoked ribs that fall off the bone, this cookbook will guide you through various grilling and smoking masterpieces.

But wait, there's more! Expand your culinary horizons with unique recipes that push the boundaries of outdoor cooking. First, picture yourself indulging in wood-fired pizzas with crispy, charred crusts and bubbling, melty cheese. Then, imagine the satisfaction of creating delectable desserts infused with the smoky essence that only the Ninja Woodfire Outdoor Grill & Smoker can provide.

So, gather your family and friends, get your Ninja Woodfire Outdoor Grill & Smoker up and running, and let this cookbook be your passport to flavor-filled adventures. Get ready to impress and delight as you unleash the full potential of your outdoor cooking.

CHAPTER 1: THE NINJA WOODFIRE OUTDOOR GRILL & SMOKER?

The Ninja Woodfire Outdoor Grill & Smoker is a remarkable cooking appliance that offers versatility and high performance to enhance your outdoor cooking experience. Designed to provide exceptional results, this appliance is perfect for various cooking styles and dishes. So whether you want to go for classic backyard grilling with burgers and hot dogs or you want to delve into the world of slow and low smoking for succulent meats, this appliance has you covered. Additionally, it goes beyond traditional grilling and smoking by offering the ability to bake pizzas, expanding your culinary possibilities.

Parts & Accessories

- Grill Plate
- Crisper Basket
- Smoke Box
- Grease Tray
- Left and Right Assembly Handles
- Socket Head Cap Screw 3.5mm x 16mm (4x) (pre-assembled on handles)
- Allen Wrench
- Pellet Scoop
- Assembled Main Unit (power cord not shown)
- Hood
- Control Panel

Function and Operate Buttons

When it comes to performance, the Ninja Woodfire Outdoor Grill & Smoker excels above all. It harnesses the power of wood-fired cooking, using wood pellets as the primary fuel source. This allows you to infuse your dishes with a distinctive smoky flavor that other cooking methods cannot replicate. In addition, the natural flavors of the wood pellets enhance the taste of your meals, giving them a delicious, smoky profile that will delight your taste buds.

Function Buttons

SMOKER: Achieve rich, smoky flavors by using slow and low cooking techniques to tenderize sizable meat cuts.

GRILL: Experience the benefits of closed-hood cooking, providing both top and bottom heat, which is ideal for grilling generous portions of meat, thick cuts, and frozen food, and achieving a perfect sear. It is recommended to open the hood while grilling for delicate foods or lean proteins. This will help achieve a delicate touch and prevent overcooking while also allowing the development of charred textures.

AIR CRISP: Attain a delightful crispy and crunchy texture using minimal to no oil and higher fan speeds.
ROAST: Effortlessly tenderize meats, roast vegetables, and accomplish various culinary tasks.

BAKE: Use lower fan speeds to prepare a delectable assortment of bread, cakes, and various other baked goods.

DEHYDRATE: Ideal for dehydrating fruits, vegetables, and jerky to perfection.

BROIL: Add a crispy finishing touch to meals or melt cheese on sandwiches.

Operating Buttons
DIAL: To turn on the appliance and choose a cooking function, rotate the dial clockwise until the desired function is selected. Conversely, to turn off the appliance, rotate the dial counterclockwise until it reaches the OFF position. When the unit is powered on, the display will be illuminated.

WOODFIRE FLAVOR TECHNOLOGY: After choosing your desired cooking function, press the button to infuse your food with the delightful Woodfire Flavor. This feature can be activated during Grill, Air Crisp, Bake, Roast, or Dehydrate functions. Upon pressing, the display screen will illuminate a flame icon.

TEMP: The default temperature setting will be shown, and if you wish to make any adjustments, you can use the - and + buttons next to the TEMP option.
TIME: For modifying the cooking duration, utilize the - and + buttons adjacent to the TIME option.

START/STOP: To initiate or halt the ongoing cooking process, press the button. Alternatively, pressing and holding the button for 3 seconds allows you to bypass the preheating stage.

Benefits of the Appliance

Dual Functionality: This appliance serves as a grill and a smoker, allowing you to explore various cooking techniques. Whether you prefer the intense grilling heat or the slow and low-smoking method, you can switch between the two effortlessly.

Wood-Fired Cooking: Harness the natural flavors of real wood with the Ninja Woodfire Outdoor Grill & Smoker. By using wood pellets as the primary fuel source, you can infuse your dishes with a rich smoky taste that other cooking methods cannot replicate.

Precise Temperature Control: Achieve the perfect cooking results every time with this grill and smoker's precise temperature control features. It includes a digital control panel that allows you to set and monitor the cooking temperature, ensuring consistent heat distribution for optimal cooking.

Ample Cooking Space: The Ninja Woodfire Outdoor Grill & Smoker offers generous cooking space, allowing you to prepare meals for large gatherings or enjoy the freedom to cook multiple dishes simultaneously. It features multiple grates and racks to accommodate various types of food.

Durable Construction: Created to withstand the rigors of outdoor cooking, this grill and smoker combo is constructed with high-quality materials. It is designed to provide long-lasting performance, from the sturdy stainless steel body to the durable grates and components.

Versatile Cooking Options: You can explore various cooking options with the Ninja Woodfire Outdoor Grill & Smoker. From traditional grilling favorites like steaks and vegetables to slow-smoked ribs and briskets, this appliance unleashes your culinary creativity.

Easy to Clean: Cleaning up after a cooking session is a breeze with this grill and smoker. It features removable components and an ash cleanout system, making it easy to maintain and keep your appliance in top shape.

How to Set Up?

If you have just bought the new Ninja Woodfire Outdoor Grill & Smoker, then after unboxing the appliance, remove and dispose of any packaging material and tape from the unit. Some stickers are meant to remain permanently attached, so only remove stickers with the label 'peel here.' Next, take out all accessories from its package and carefully read this manual. It is best to wash all the accessories with water, dry and place them back before the first use.

Handle Installation:
Make sure to correctly utilize the appropriate handle on both the left and right sides. You will find an Allen wrench attached to the left handle with tape. When placing the unit on a table, either position it at the edge or, if the lid is still taped down, carefully flip the grill upside down by grasping the sides of the unit and holding the lid down. If the tape has been removed, remove all accessories from the grill. While holding the sides of the unit and keeping the lid down, position the grill on top of the top pulp tray piece to protect the unit. Align each handle with the corresponding tabs on the base, then push upward to secure each handle in place. Finally, utilize the provided Allen wrench to tighten pre-assembled screws (2x) on each handle.

Extension Cord:
When using extension cords, it's crucial to prioritize safety and efficiency. Outdoor extension cords should be specifically designed for outdoor use, marked with "SJOW" and labeled as suitable for outdoor appliances. Select the appropriate cord length (up to 25 feet with 14-gauge or up to 50 feet with 12-gauge) to avoid overheating, melting, and voltage drops. Following these guidelines ensures optimal performance and minimizes potential risks associated with electrical hazards.

Installing the Removable Smoke Box:
The unit is equipped with a pre-installed smoke box on the lid's right side. Therefore, prior to adding pellets, it is essential to confirm that the removable smoke box is inserted correctly. For installation, use one hand to keep the smoke box lid open while inserting the removable smoke box into its designated position.

Adding Ninja Woodfire Pellets:
To prevent any spillage, fill the pellet scoop to its maximum capacity and ensure the pellets are leveled off. While holding the smoke box lid open, carefully pour the pellets into the smoke box until it reaches the top, then close the lid securely. Before starting the cooking process, double-check that the lid is closed correctly. It is recommended to use Ninja Woodfire Pellets exclusively for optimal results, performance, and flavor.

Removing the Smoke Box and Cleaning:
To prevent any burns, allow the pellets to burn completely and let the smoke box cool down. Once this is done, remove the smoke box and carefully dispose of its contents.

How to Use it?

Smoke
Before starting, make sure that the grill is positioned

on a flat and level surface. Open the hood and install the grill plate by placing it flat on top of the heating element, ensuring it sits securely. Slide the grease tray into position at the back of the grill. Lift the smoke box lid, and using the pellet scoop, fill it with pellets until it reaches the top, being cautious not to overfill. Finally, securely close the the smoke box lid.

Begin by opening the hood and arranging the ingredients on the grill plate. Once done, close the hood securely. Ensure that the grill is connected to a power source, and then turn the dial in a clockwise direction from the OFF position to select the SMOKER function. The default temperature setting will be displayed. Utilize the - and + buttons next to the TEMP option to select a desired temperature ranging from 250°F to 410°F in increments of 10 degrees. Similarly, adjust the cooking time by using the - and + buttons next to the TIME option. For example, you can set the cooking time from 1 minute to 30 minutes in 1-minute increments or from 30 minutes to 12 hours in 15-minute increments.

Initiate the cooking process by pressing the START button. The Smoker function does not require any preheating time. Once the set cook time elapses, the unit will emit a beep sound, and the display will show "DONE." Proceed to remove the food from the grill plate.

Grill
Position the grill on a flat and level surface. Open the hood and securely install the grill plate by placing it flat on top of the heating element, ensuring it sits cor-

rectly. Slide the grease tray into place at the back of the grill.

If you intend to utilize the Woodfire Flavor Technology, lift the smoke box lid. Fill the smoke box with pellets up to the top using the pellet scoop. Remember not to overfill the smoke box. Close the smoke box lid. Ensure that the grill is connected to a power source. Rotate the dial clockwise from the OFF position to select the GRILL function. If you wish to add Woodfire Flavor Technology, press the dedicated WOODFIRE FLAVOR button.

The default temperature setting will be displayed. Next, use the - and + buttons adjacent to the TEMP option to select a temperature ranging from LO to HI. Next, utilize the - and + buttons next to the TIME option to adjust the cooking time, increasing or decreasing in 1-minute increments, up to a maximum of 1 hour. Finally, push the START button to commence the preheating process. If you have chosen to use Woodfire Flavor Technology, the pellets will undergo an ignition cycle (IGN) before the grill begins preheating (PRE).

When the preheating phase is complete, the unit will emit a beep sound, and the display will show "ADD FOOD." Next, open the hood and place the ingredients on the grill plate. The cooking process will commence once the hood is closed, and the timer will start counting down. When the set cook time reaches zero, the grill will emit a beep sound, and the display will show "DONE." Proceed to remove the food from the grill plate.

Cooking with Other Options
To use the other cooking options, you must set up this grill and smoker according to the instructions mentioned in the previous sections. For example, if you want to air fry or roast the food, then position the crisper basket on the grill plate, aligning the basket feet with the designated indentations on the surface of the grill plate.

Then slide the grease tray into position at the back of the grill. If you intend to add Woodfire Flavor, lift the smoke box lid. Use the given scoop to fill the smoke box with pellets, ensuring they reach the top. Close the smoke box lid, taking care not to overfill it.

Make sure the grill is connected to a power source. Rotate the dial clockwise from the OFF position to select the AIR CRISP/ ROAST/ BAKE/ DEHYDRATE/ BROIL function. If you wish to incorporate Woodfire

Flavor, press the dedicated WOODFIRE FLAVOR TECHNOLOGY button. (NOTE: Woodfire Flavor Technology cannot be used with the Broil function.) The default temperature setting will be displayed according to the preset settings for each program function. To select a desired temperature, utilize the - and + buttons next to the TEMP option. Use the - and + buttons next to the TIME option to adjust the cooking time.

Press the START button to initiate the preheating process. If you have chosen to use Woodfire Flavor Technology, the pellets will undergo an ignition cycle (IGN) before the grill commences preheating (PRE). Preheating is strongly recommended for optimal results, but you can skip this step by pressing and holding the START/STOP key for 4 seconds. When the preheating phase is complete, the unit will emit a beep sound, and the display will show "ADD FOOD."
Open the hood and place the ingredients on the crisper basket/grill plate. Cooking will commence once the hood is closed, and the timer will begin counting down. When the set cook time elapses, the unit will beep, and the display will show "DONE." Safely remove the food from the appliance.

Cleaning Your Woodfire Electric BBQ Grill & Smoker

After each use, it is essential to clean the unit thoroughly. Always allow both the appliance and accessories to cool down before starting the cleaning process. Before cleaning, make sure to unplug the unit from the power source. Keep its hood open after removing your food to expedite the cooling process.

Remove the smoke box and safely dispose of the cooled ash contents after every use for proper maintenance. The pellet scoop can be cleaned in the dishwasher. However, please note that the grill plate, grease tray, crisper basket, and smoke box should not be placed in the dishwasher.

Carefully take out the cooled grease tray from the back of the unit. Safely discard the grease contents; with warm and soapy water, try to hand-wash the grease tray. Before storing or removing the grease tray, inspect the bottom of the unit for any debris buildup and wipe it clean with a damp cloth. Avoid using chemicals for this process. You don't need to clean your smoke box after every use is not required. But I recommend using a stiff brush to remove any excess creosote buildup after every ten uses.

If any food particles, residue, or grease are stuck on the grill plate or any other removable part, soak them in warm, soapy water before cleaning. After each use, remove the non-stick grill plate and, if used, the crisper basket, and hand-wash them with warm, soapy water. When storing the coated accessories, it is advisable to stack them while placing a cloth or paper towel between each piece to protect the coated surfaces. Wipe down the inner portion with a damp towel or cloth after each use to clean the hood. This will help deodorize the unit and remove any grease residue.

Common Tools for Outdoor Grill

When it comes to outdoor grilling, having the right tools at your disposal can make your cooking experience more enjoyable and efficient. Here are some standard tools that are essential for outdoor grilling:

Grill Brush: A grill brush with sturdy bristles is essential for cleaning the grates before and after cooking. In addition, it helps to remove any leftover food particles or debris, ensuring a clean cooking surface.

Tongs: Long-handled tongs are versatile and valuable for flipping meats, vegetables, and other food items on the grill. Look for tongs with a firm grip and heat-resistant handles.

Spatula: Choosing a spatula with a long handle enables effortless maneuvering and prevents fragile foods such as fish fillets or burgers from breaking when flipped. A practical option is a broad and durable spatula, ideal for this purpose.

Grill Fork: A grill fork with long tines is helpful for

piercing and lifting larger cuts of meat, such as whole hens, chickens, or roasts. It can also be used for testing the doneness of thicker cuts by inserting the fork into the meat.

Grilling Gloves: Heat-resistant grilling gloves are essential for protecting your hands and forearms from the intense heat of the grill. They allow you to safely handle hot utensils, adjust charcoal or wood, and move food around the grill.

Grill Light: A grill light is helpful for nighttime grilling or cooking in low-light conditions. It attaches to the grill handle or clamp and illuminates the cooking surface, making it easier to see and monitor your food.

Meat Thermometer: A reliable meat thermometer ensures that your grilled meats are cooked to the desired level of doneness. It helps you avoid undercooking or overcooking, ensuring safe and flavorful results.

Grill Basket: A grill basket is ideal for cooking smaller or delicate items like vegetables, seafood, or even small cuts of meat. It prevents them from falling through the grates while allowing them to cook evenly.

Basting Brush: It has heat-resistant bristles to apply liquids to the food. Look for brushes with long handles for easy reach.

Aluminum Foil: Aluminum foil is a versatile tool for grilling. It can be used to create makeshift drip pans, wrap vegetables or fish for cooking, or even cover and let meats rest after grilling.

Safety Precautions for Outdoor Grill

Safety always comes first when it comes to outdoor grilling. Although the Ninja Woodfire Outdoor Grill and Smoker are entirely automated and offer several safety features, you still need to use this appliance cautiously. So make sure to keep the following precautionary measures in mind while using this appliance:

- Ensure that the pellets in the pellet box do not overflow. Overflowing pellets can introduce oxygen, leading to combustion, flames, and damage to the unit. This can potentially cause burn injuries.
- Refrain from touching the accessories during or immediately after cooking. The basket becomes extremely hot during the cooking process. Exercise caution when removing the accessory from the appliance to avoid burns or personal injury. I recommend using long-handled utensils and protective hot pads or insulated oven gloves.
- Always ensure the grill is completely cool before releasing and removing the cooking plates or moving them to another location. This precaution is necessary to prevent burns or personal injury.
- Do not use the appliance without installing the grill plate. The grill plate is an essential component for safe operation.
- To protect against electric shock, arrange the cord and extension cord to prevent them from draping over the countertop or table where they pose a tripping hazard. Keep the cord connection dry and avoid immersing the cord, plugs, or main unit housing in water or liquid.
- Regularly inspect the appliance and power cord for any damage. Do not use the appliance if the power cord or plug shows signs of damage. In case of any malfunction or damage to the appliance, immediately discontinue use and contact Customer Service.
- Never use the socket located below the countertop surface.
- Avoid connecting this appliance to an external timer switch or a separate remote-control system.

CHAPTER 2: BREAKFAST

Crust-Less Quiche

SERVES: 2

Cooking spray
4 eggs
1 cup Gouda cheese, shredded
½ cup tomatoes, chopped
¼ cup onion, chopped
½ cup milk
Salt, to taste

1. Grease 2 ramekins with cooking spray lightly.
2. Mix together all the ingredients in ramekins until well combined.
3. To install the grill grate, position it flat on top of the heating element and gently press down until it sits into place, then close the hood. Turn dial to BAKE, set temperature to 340°F, set time to 30 minutes. Select START/STOP to begin preheating (preheating will take approx. 3 minutes).
4. When unit beeps to signify it is preheated and ADD FOOD is displayed, open hood and place ramekins on grill grate. Close hood to begin cooking.
5. When cooking is complete, open hood and carefully remove the ramekins. Serve hot.

PREP: 5 minutes
PREHEAT: approx. 3 minutes
TOTAL COOK TIME: 30 minutes

Breakfast Zucchini

SERVES: 4

4 zucchinis, diced into 1-inch pieces, drained
2 small onion, chopped medium
2 small bell pepper, chopped medium
Pinch salt and black pepper

1. To install the grill grate, position it flat on top of the heating element and gently press down until it sits into place. Place Air Crisp Basket on grill grate, then close the hood.
2. While holding the smoke box lid open, use the pellet scoop to pour pellets into the smoke box until filled to the top. Then close the smoke box lid.
3. Turn dial to ROAST. Press WOODFIRE FLAVOR. Set temperature to 390°F, and set time to 15 minutes. Select START/STOP to begin preheating (preheating will take approx. 8–10 minutes).
4. Season the zucchini, onion and bell pepper with salt and black pepper.
5. When unit beeps to signify it has preheated and ADD FOOD is displayed, open hood and place vegetables in basket. Close hood to begin cooking.
6. With 7 minutes remaining, open hood and use silicone-tipped tongs to flip the vegetables.
7. When cooking is complete, open hood, remove vegetables from basket, and serve warm.

PREP: 5 minutes
PREHEAT: approx. 8-10 minutes
TOTAL COOK TIME: 15 minutes

Bacon and Hot Dogs Omelet

SERVES: 2

PREP: 10 minutes
PREHEAT: approx. 3 minutes
TOTAL COOK TIME: 10 minutes

1 tbsp. unsalted butter, melted
4 eggs
1 bacon slice, chopped
2 hot dogs, chopped
2 small onions, chopped
2 tbsps. milk
Salt and black pepper, to taste

1. Grease a round baking pan with butter.
2. Whisk together eggs and stir in the remaining ingredients.
3. Stir well to combine and place in the baking pan.
4. To install the grill grate, position it flat on top of the heating element and gently press down until it sits into place, then close the hood. Turn dial to BAKE, set temperature to 325°F, set time to 10 minutes. Select START/STOP to begin preheating (preheating will take approx. 3 minutes).
5. When unit beeps to signify it is preheated and ADD FOOD is displayed, open hood and place baking pan on grill grate. Close hood to begin cooking.
6. When cooking is complete, open hood and carefully remove the baking pan. Cool the omelet slightly before serving.

Cream Cheese Cupcakes

SERVES: 10

PREP: 10 minutes
PREHEAT: approx. 3 minutes
TOTAL COOK TIME: 20 minutes

4½-ounce self-rising flour
4¾-ounce butter, softened
½-ounce cream cheese, softened
½ cup fresh raspberries

2 eggs
4¼-ounce caster sugar
2 tsps. fresh lemon juice
Pinch of salt

1. Grease 10 silicon cups.
2. Mix flour, baking powder and salt in a bowl.
3. Combine cream cheese, sugar, eggs and butter in another bowl.
4. Mix the flour mixture with the cream cheese mixture and squeeze in the lemon juice.
5. Transfer the mixture into 10 silicon cups and top each cup with 2 raspberries.
6. To install the grill grate, position it flat on top of the heating element and gently press down until it sits into place, then close the hood. Turn dial to BAKE, set temperature to 365°F, set time to 20 minutes. Select START/STOP to begin preheating (preheating will take approx. 3 minutes).
7. When unit beeps to signify it is preheated and ADD FOOD is displayed, open hood and place silicon cups on grill grate. Close hood to begin cooking.
8. When cooking is complete, open hood and carefully remove the cupcakes from the grill. Serve warm.

Cinnamon Banana Bread

SERVES: 8

½ cup olive oil
3 bananas, peeled and sliced
½ cup milk
⅔ cup sugar
1 tbsp. unsalted butter, melted

1⅓ cups flour
1 tsp. baking soda
1 tsp. baking powder
1 tsp. ground cinnamon
1 tsp. salt

PREP: 10 minutes
PREHEAT: approx. 3 minutes
TOTAL COOK TIME: 20 minutes

1. Grease a loaf pan with butter.
2. Mix together all the dry ingredients with the wet ingredients to form a dough.
3. Place the dough into the prepared loaf pan.
4. To install the grill grate, position it flat on top of the heating element and gently press down until it sits into place, then close the hood. Turn dial to BAKE, set temperature to 330°F, set time to 20 minutes. Select START/STOP to begin preheating (preheating will take approx. 3 minutes).
5. When unit beeps to signify it is preheated and ADD FOOD is displayed, open hood and place loaf pan on grill grate. Close hood to begin cooking.
6. When cooking is complete, open hood and carefully remove the bread from the grill. Cut the bread into desired size slices and serve warm.

Pumpkin and Yogurt Bread

SERVES: 4

1 tbsp. unsalted butter, melted
8 tbsps. pumpkin puree
2 large eggs
6 tbsps. banana flour
6 tbsps. oats

4 tbsps. plain Greek yogurt
4 tbsps. honey
2 tbsps. vanilla essence
Pinch of ground nutmeg

PREP: 10 minutes
PREHEAT: approx. 3 minutes
TOTAL COOK TIME: 15 minutes

1. Grease a loaf pan with butter.
2. Mix together all the ingredients except oats in a bowl and beat with the hand mixer until smooth.
3. Add oats and mix until well combined. Transfer the mixture into the prepared loaf pan.
4. To install the grill grate, position it flat on top of the heating element and gently press down until it sits into place, then close the hood. Turn dial to BAKE, set temperature to 360°F, set time to 15 minutes. Select START/STOP to begin preheating (preheating will take approx. 3 minutes).
5. When unit beeps to signify it is preheated and ADD FOOD is displayed, open hood and place loaf pan on grill grate. Close hood to begin cooking.
6. When cooking is complete, open hood and carefully remove the bread from the grill. Place onto a wire rack to cool and cut the bread into desired size slices to serve.

Nutty Fudge Muffins

SERVES: 10

PREP: 5 minutes
PREHEAT: approx. 3 minutes
TOTAL COOK TIME: 10 minutes

1 package fudge brownie mix
1 egg
2 tsps. water
¼ cup walnuts, chopped
⅓ cup vegetable oil

1. Grease 10 muffin tins lightly.
2. Mix brownie mix, egg, oil and water in a bowl.
3. Fold in the walnuts and pour the mixture in the muffin cups.
4. To install the grill grate, position it flat on top of the heating element and gently press down until it sits into place, then close the hood. Turn dial to BAKE, set temperature to 300°F, set time to 10 minutes. Select START/STOP to begin preheating (preheating will take approx. 3 minutes).
5. When unit beeps to signify it is preheated and ADD FOOD is displayed, open hood and place muffin tins on grill grate. Close hood to begin cooking.
6. When cooking is complete, open hood and carefully remove the muffins. Serve hot.

Ham and Egg Toast Cups

SERVES: 2

PREP: 5 minutes
PREHEAT: approx. 8-10 minutes
TOTAL COOK TIME: 5 minutes

2 eggs
2 slices of ham
2 tbsps. Butter, melted
Cheddar cheese, for topping
Salt, to taste
Black pepper, to taste

1. Grease both ramekins with melted butter.
2. Place each ham slice in the greased ramekins and crack each egg over ham slices.
3. Sprinkle with salt, black pepper and cheddar cheese.
4. To install the grill grate, position it flat on top of the heating element and gently press down until it sits into place, then close the hood.
5. While holding the smoke box lid open, use the pellet scoop to pour pellets into the smoke box until filled to the top. Then close the smoke box lid.
6. Turn dial to BAKE. Press WOODFIRE FLAVOR. Set temperature to 400°F, and set time to 5 minutes. Select START/STOP to begin preheating (preheating will take approx. 8–10 minutes).
7. When unit beeps to signify it has preheated and ADD FOOD is displayed, open hood and place ramekins on grill grate. Close hood to begin cooking.
8. When cooking is complete, open hood and remove the ramekins. Serve warm.

Crispy Potato Rosti

1 tbsp. vegetable oil
½ pound russet potatoes, peeled and grated roughly
⅛ cup cheddar cheese
1 tbsp. chives, chopped finely

2 tbsps. shallots, minced
3.5 ounces smoked salmon, cut into slices
2 tbsps. sour cream
Salt and black pepper, to taste

PREP: 10 minutes
PREHEAT: approx. 8-10 minutes
TOTAL COOK TIME: 15 minutes

1. Grease a pizza pan with the vegetable oil.
2. Mix together potatoes, shallots, chives, cheese, salt and black pepper in a large bowl until well combined. Transfer the potato mixture into the prepared pizza pan.
3. To install the grill grate, position it flat on top of the heating element and gently press down until it sits into place, then close the hood.
4. While holding the smoke box lid open, use the pellet scoop to pour pellets into the smoke box until filled to the top. Then close the smoke box lid.
5. Turn dial to BAKE. Press WOODFIRE FLAVOR. Set temperature to 365°F, and set time to 15 minutes. Select START/STOP to begin preheating (preheating will take approx. 8–10 minutes).
6. When unit beeps to signify it has preheated and ADD FOOD is displayed, open hood and place pizza pan on grill grate. Close hood to begin cooking.
7. When cooking is complete, open hood and remove the potato rosti. Cut the potato rosti into wedges and top with smoked salmon slices and sour cream to serve.

Crispy Breakfast Frittata

¼ pound breakfast sausage, fully cooked and crumbled
4 eggs, lightly beaten
½ cup Monterey Jack cheese, shredded
2 tbsps. red bell pepper, diced
1 green onion, chopped
1 pinch cayenne pepper

PREP: 15 minutes
PREHEAT: approx. 3 minutes
TOTAL COOK TIME: 20 minutes

1. Grease a nonstick 6x2-inch cake pan.
2. Whisk together eggs with sausage, green onion, bell pepper, cheese and cayenne in a bowl.
3. Transfer the egg mixture in the prepared cake pan.
4. To install the grill grate, position it flat on top of the heating element and gently press down until it sits into place, then close the hood. Turn dial to BAKE, set temperature to 365°F, set time to 20 minutes. Select START/STOP to begin preheating (preheating will take approx. 3 minutes).
5. When unit beeps to signify it is preheated and ADD FOOD is displayed, open hood and place cake pan on grill grate. Close hood to begin cooking.
6. When cooking is complete, open hood and carefully remove the cake pan. Serve warm.

Yummy Savory French Toasts

SERVES: 2

PREP: 10 minutes
PREHEAT: approx. 10-12 minutes
TOTAL COOK TIME: 4 minutes

¼ cup chickpea flour
3 tbsps. onion, chopped finely
2 tsps. green chili, seeded and chopped finely
Water, as required
4 bread slices
½ tsp. red chili powder
¼ tsp. ground turmeric
¼ tsp. ground cumin
Salt, to taste

1. To install the grill grate, position it flat on top of the heating element and gently press down until it sits into place, then close the hood. Turn dial to GRILL, set temperature to HI, and set time to 4 minutes. Select START/STOP to begin cooking (preheating will take approx. 10–12 minutes).
2. Mix together all the ingredients in a large bowl except the bread slices. Spread the mixture over both sides of the bread slices.
3. When the unit has beeped to signify it has preheated and ADD FOOD is displayed, open the hood, and place the bread slices on the grill, close hood, and cook for 2 minutes per side or until bread is toasted and grill marks are prevalent.
4. When cooking is complete, open hood, remove bread from grill and serve warm.

Doughnuts Pudding

SERVES: 4

PREP: 15 minutes
PREHEAT: approx. 3 minutes
TOTAL COOK TIME: 1 hour

6 glazed doughnuts, cut into small pieces
4 egg yolks
1½ cups whipping cream
¾ cup frozen sweet cherries
½ cup semi-sweet chocolate baking chips
½ cup raisins
¼ cup sugar
1 tsp. ground cinnamon

1. Grease a baking dish lightly.
2. Mix doughnut pieces, cherries, raisins, chocolate chips, sugar, and cinnamon in a large bowl.
3. Whisk the egg yolks with whipping cream in another bowl until well combined.
4. Combine the egg yolk mixture into the doughnut mixture and mix well.
5. Arrange the doughnuts mixture evenly into the baking dish.
6. To install the grill grate, position it flat on top of the heating element and gently press down until it sits into place, then close the hood. Turn dial to BAKE, set temperature to 310°F, set time to 60 minutes. Select START/STOP to begin preheating (preheating will take approx. 3 minutes).
7. When unit beeps to signify it is preheated and ADD FOOD is displayed, open hood and place baking dish on grill grate. Close hood to begin cooking.
8. When cooking is complete, open hood and carefully remove the baking dish. Serve hot.

Zucchini Fritters

SERVES: 4

10½ ounces zucchini, grated and squeezed
7 ounces Halloumi cheese
¼ cup all-purpose flour
2 eggs
1 tsp. fresh dill, minced
Salt and black pepper, to taste

PREP: 15 minutes
PREHEAT: approx. 8-10 minutes
TOTAL COOK TIME: 12 minutes

1. Mix together all the ingredients in a large bowl. Make small fritters from this mixture.
2. To install the grill grate, position it flat on top of the heating element and gently press down until it sits into place. Place Air Crisp Basket on grill grate, then close the hood.
3. While holding the smoke box lid open, use the pellet scoop to pour pellets into the smoke box until filled to the top. Then close the smoke box lid.
4. Turn dial to AIR CRISP. Press WOODFIRE FLAVOR. Set temperature to 390°F, and set time to 12 minutes. Select START/STOP to begin preheating (preheating will take approx. 8–10 minutes).
5. When unit beeps to signify it has preheated and ADD FOOD is displayed, open hood and place fritters in basket. Close hood to begin cooking.
6. With 6 minutes remaining, open hood and use silicone-tipped tongs to flip the fritters.
7. When cooking is complete, open hood, remove fritters from basket, and serve warm.

Mini Tomato Quiche

SERVES: 2

1 tbsp. unsalted butter, melted
4 eggs
1 cup Cheddar cheese, shredded
½ cup tomatoes, chopped
2 asparagus spears, chopped
½ cup milk
Salt, to taste

PREP: 15 minutes
PREHEAT: approx. 3 minutes
TOTAL COOK TIME: 20 minutes

1. Grease a large ramekin with butter.
2. Mix together all the ingredients in a ramekin.
3. To install the grill grate, position it flat on top of the heating element and gently press down until it sits into place, then close the hood. Turn dial to BAKE, set temperature to 340°F, set time to 20 minutes. Select START/STOP to begin preheating (preheating will take approx. 3 minutes).
4. When unit beeps to signify it is preheated and ADD FOOD is displayed, open hood and place ramekin on grill grate. Close hood to begin cooking.
5. When cooking is complete, open hood and carefully remove the quiche. Cool on a wire rack prior to serving.

Flavorful Bacon Cups

SERVES: 6

PREP: 10 minutes
PREHEAT: approx. 8-10 minutes
TOTAL COOK TIME: 15 minutes

6 bacon slices
6 bread slices
1 scallion, chopped
3 tbsps. green bell pepper, seeded and chopped
6 eggs
2 tbsps. low-fat mayonnaise
Cooking spray

1. Grease 6 cups muffin tin with cooking spray.
2. Place each bacon slice in a prepared muffin cup.
3. Cut the bread slices with round cookie cutter and place over the bacon slices.
4. Top with bell pepper, scallion and mayonnaise evenly and crack 1 egg in each muffin cup.
5. To install the grill grate, position it flat on top of the heating element and gently press down until it sits into place, then close the hood.
6. While holding the smoke box lid open, use the pellet scoop to pour pellets into the smoke box until filled to the top. Then close the smoke box lid.
7. Turn dial to BAKE. Press WOODFIRE FLAVOR. Set temperature to 375°F, and set time to 15 minutes. Select START/STOP to begin preheating (preheating will take approx. 8–10 minutes).
8. When unit beeps to signify it has preheated and ADD FOOD is displayed, open hood and place muffin cups on grill grate. Close hood to begin cooking.
9. When cooking is complete, open hood and remove the muffin cups. Serve warm.

CHAPTER 3: VEGETABLES

Jalapeño Poppers

SERVES: 4

8 medium jalapeño peppers
5 ounces (142 g) cream cheese
¼ cup grated Mozzarella cheese

½ tsp. Italian seasoning mix
8 slices bacon

PREP: 5 minutes
PREHEAT: approx. 8-10 minutes
TOTAL COOK TIME: 16 minutes

1. Cut the jalapeños in half. Use a spoon to scrape out the insides of the peppers.
2. In a bowl, add together the cream cheese, Mozzarella cheese and Italian seasoning.
3. Pack the cream cheese mixture into the jalapeño halves and place the other halves on top.
4. Wrap each pepper in 1 slice of bacon, starting from the bottom and working up.
5. To install the grill grate, position it flat on top of the heating element and gently press down until it sits into place. Place Air Crisp Basket on grill grate, then close the hood.
6. While holding the smoke box lid open, use the pellet scoop to pour pellets into the smoke box until filled to the top. Then close the smoke box lid.
7. Turn dial to BROIL. Press WOODFIRE FLAVOR. Set temperature to 390°F, and set time to 16 minutes. Select START/STOP to begin preheating (preheating will take approx. 8–10 minutes).
8. When unit beeps to signify it has preheated and ADD FOOD is displayed, open hood and place the peppers in basket. Close hood to begin cooking.
9. When cooking is complete, open hood, remove the peppers from basket. Let cool slightly before serving.

Grilled Broccoli and Arugula Salad

SERVES: 4

2 heads broccoli, trimmed into florets
½ red onion, sliced
1 tbsp. canola oil
2 tbsps. extra-virgin olive oil
1 tbsp. freshly squeezed lemon juice
1 tsp. honey

1 tsp. Dijon mustard
1 garlic clove, minced
Pinch red pepper flakes
¼ tsp. fine sea salt
Freshly ground black pepper
4 cups arugula, torn
2 tbsps. grated Parmesan cheese

PREP: 10 minutes
PREHEAT: approx. 15-19 minutes
TOTAL COOK TIME: 20 minutes

1. In a large bowl, combine the broccoli, sliced onion, and canola oil and toss until coated.
2. To install the grill grate, position it flat on top of the heating element and gently press down until it sits into place, then close the hood.
3. While holding the smoke box lid open, use the pellet scoop to pour pellets into the smoke box until filled to the top. Then close the smoke box lid.
4. Turn dial to GRILL. Press WOODFIRE FLAVOR. Set temperature to HI, and set time to 20 minutes. Select START/STOP to begin preheating (preheating will take approx. 15–19 minutes).
5. When unit beeps to signify it has preheated and ADD FOOD is displayed, open hood and place the broccoli and onion on grill grate, gently pressing them down to maximize grill marks. Close hood to begin cooking, tossing frequently during cooking.
6. Meanwhile, in a medium bowl, whisk together the olive oil, lemon juice, honey, mustard, garlic, red pepper flakes, salt, and pepper.
7. With 10 minutes remaining, open hood and set the onion aside to cool.
8. When cooking is complete, open hood, remove the broccoli from grill. Combine the grilled broccoli and onion with arugula in a large serving bowl. Drizzle with the vinaigrette to taste, and sprinkle with the Parmesan cheese.

Cashew Stuffed Mushrooms

SERVES: 6

PREP: 10 minutes
PREHEAT: approx. 8-10 minutes
TOTAL COOK TIME: 12 minutes

1 pound (454 g) baby Bella mushroom, stems removed
1 cup basil
½ cup cashew, soaked overnight
½ cup nutritional yeast
1 tbsp. lemon juice
2 cloves garlic
1 tbsp. olive oil
Salt, to taste

1. Prepare the pesto. In a food processor, blend the basil, cashew nuts, nutritional yeast, lemon juice, garlic and olive oil to combine well. Sprinkle with salt as desired.
2. Turn the mushrooms cap-side down and spread the pesto on the underside of each cap.
3. To install the grill grate, position it flat on top of the heating element and gently press down until it sits into place. Place Air Crisp Basket on grill grate, then close the hood.
4. While holding the smoke box lid open, use the pellet scoop to pour pellets into the smoke box until filled to the top. Then close the smoke box lid.
5. Turn dial to AIR CRISP. Press WOODFIRE FLAVOR. Set temperature to 400°F, and set time to 12 minutes. Select START/STOP to begin preheating (preheating will take approx. 8–10 minutes).
6. When unit beeps to signify it has preheated and ADD FOOD is displayed, open hood and place the mushrooms in basket. Close hood to begin cooking.
7. When cooking is complete, open hood, remove the mushrooms from basket. Let cool slightly before serving.

Cheesy Potato Patties

SERVES: 8

PREP: 5 minutes
PREHEAT: approx. 8-10 minutes
TOTAL COOK TIME: 10 minutes

2 pounds (907 g) white potatoes
2 cups shredded Colby cheese
1 cup crushed crackers
½ cup finely chopped scallions
½ tsp. freshly ground black pepper, or more to taste
1 tbsp. fine sea salt
½ tsp. hot paprika
¼ cup canola oil

1. Boil the potatoes until soft. Dry them off and peel them before mashing thoroughly, leaving no lumps.
2. Combine the mashed potatoes with scallions, pepper, salt, paprika, and cheese.
3. Mold the mixture into balls with your hands and press with your palm to flatten them into patties.
4. In a shallow dish, combine the canola oil and crushed crackers. Coat the patties in the crumb mixture.
5. To install the grill grate, position it flat on top of the heating element and gently press down until it sits into place. Place Air Crisp Basket on grill grate, then close the hood.
6. While holding the smoke box lid open, use the pellet scoop to pour pellets into the smoke box until filled to the top. Then close the smoke box lid.
7. Turn dial to AIR CRISP. Press WOODFIRE FLAVOR. Set temperature to 390°F, and set time to 10 minutes. Select START/STOP to begin preheating (preheating will take approx. 8–10 minutes).
8. When unit beeps to signify it has preheated and ADD FOOD is displayed, open hood and place the patties in basket. Close hood to begin cooking.
9. With 5 minutes remaining, open hood and use silicone-tipped tongs to flip the patties.
10. When cooking is complete, open hood, remove the patties from basket, and serve.

Cheesy Ranch Cauliflower Steaks

SERVES: 2

1 head cauliflower, stemmed
and leaves removed
¼ cup canola oil
½ tsp. garlic powder
½ tsp. paprika
Sea salt

Freshly ground black pepper
1 cup shredded Cheddar cheese
Ranch dressing, for garnish
4 slices bacon, cooked and crumbled
2 tbsps. chopped fresh chives

PREP: 10 minutes
PREHEAT: approx. 15-19 minutes
TOTAL COOK TIME: 15 minutes

1. Cut the cauliflower from top to bottom into two 2-inch "steaks"; reserve the remaining cauliflower to cook separately.
2. In a small bowl, whisk together the oil, garlic powder, and paprika. Season with salt and pepper. Brush each steak with the oil mixture on both sides.
3. To install the grill grate, position it flat on top of the heating element and gently press down until it sits into place, then close the hood.
4. While holding the smoke box lid open, use the pellet scoop to pour pellets into the smoke box until filled to the top. Then close the smoke box lid.
5. Turn dial to GRILL. Press WOODFIRE FLAVOR. Set temperature to HI, and set time to 15 minutes. Select START/STOP to begin preheating (preheating will take approx. 15–19 minutes).
6. When unit beeps to signify it has preheated and ADD FOOD is displayed, open hood and place the steaks on grill grate, gently pressing them down to maximize grill marks. Close the hood and grill for 10 minutes. Then open hood, flip the steaks and top each with ½ cup of cheese. Grill for another 5 minutes.
7. When cooking is complete, open hood. Remove the steaks from grill and drizzle with the ranch dressing. Top with the bacon and chives.

Carrot and Celery Croquettes

SERVES: 4

2 medium-sized carrots, trimmed
and grated
2 medium-sized celery stalks,
trimmed and grated
½ cup finely chopped leek
1 tbsp. garlic paste
¼ tsp. freshly cracked black pepper

1 tsp. fine sea salt
1 tbsp. finely chopped fresh dill
1 egg, lightly whisked
¼ cup whole wheat flour
¼ tsp. baking powder
½ cup bread crumbs
Cooking spray
Chive mayo, for serving

PREP: 10 minutes
PREHEAT: approx. 8-10 minutes
TOTAL COOK TIME: 6 minutes

1. Drain any excess liquid from the carrots and celery by placing them on a paper towel.
2. Stir together the vegetables with all of the other ingredients, save for the bread crumbs and chive mayo.
3. Use your hands to mold 1 tbsp. of the vegetable mixture into a ball and repeat until all of the mixture has been used up. Press down on each ball with your hand or a palette knife. Cover completely with bread crumbs. Spritz the croquettes with cooking spray.
4. To install the grill grate, position it flat on top of the heating element and gently press down until it sits into place. Place Air Crisp Basket on grill grate, then close the hood.
5. While holding the smoke box lid open, use the pellet scoop to pour pellets into the smoke box until filled to the top. Then close the smoke box lid.
6. Turn dial to AIR CRISP. Press WOODFIRE FLAVOR. Set temperature to 390°F, and set time to 6 minutes. Select START/STOP to begin preheating (preheating will take approx. 8–10 minutes).
7. When unit beeps to signify it has preheated and ADD FOOD is displayed, open hood and place the croquettes in basket. Close hood to begin cooking.
8. With 3 minutes remaining, open hood and use silicone-tipped tongs to flip the croquettes.
9. When cooking is complete, open hood, remove the croquettes from basket, and serve warm with the chive mayo on the side.

Sriracha Golden Cauliflower

SERVES: 4

PREP: 5 minutes
PREHEAT: approx. 8-10 minutes
TOTAL COOK TIME: 17 minutes

¼ cup vegan butter, melted
¼ cup sriracha sauce
4 cups cauliflower florets

1 cup bread crumbs
1 tsp. salt

1. Mix the sriracha and vegan butter in a bowl and pour this mixture over the cauliflower, taking care to cover each floret entirely.
2. In a separate bowl, combine the bread crumbs and salt.
3. Dip the cauliflower florets in the bread crumbs, coating each one well.
4. To install the grill grate, position it flat on top of the heating element and gently press down until it sits into place. Place Air Crisp Basket on grill grate, then close the hood.
5. While holding the smoke box lid open, use the pellet scoop to pour pellets into the smoke box until filled to the top. Then close the smoke box lid.
6. Turn dial to ROAST. Press WOODFIRE FLAVOR. Set temperature to 375°F, and set time to 17 minutes. Select START/STOP to begin preheating (preheating will take approx. 8–10 minutes).
7. When unit beeps to signify it has preheated and ADD FOOD is displayed, open hood and place the cauliflower florets in basket. Close hood to begin cooking.
8. With 8 minutes remaining, open hood and use silicone-tipped tongs to flip the cauliflower florets.
9. When cooking is complete, open hood, remove the cauliflower florets from basket, and serve.

Marinara Pepperoni Mushroom Pizza

SERVES: 4

PREP: 5 minutes
PREHEAT: approx. 8-10 minutes
TOTAL COOK TIME: 15 minutes

4 large portobello mushrooms, stems removed
4 tsps. olive oil
1 cup marinara sauce
1 cup shredded Mozzarella cheese
10 slices sugar-free pepperoni

1. Brush each mushroom cap with the olive oil, one tsp. for each cap.
2. To install the grill grate, position it flat on top of the heating element and gently press down until it sits into place. Place Air Crisp Basket on grill grate, then close the hood.
3. While holding the smoke box lid open, use the pellet scoop to pour pellets into the smoke box until filled to the top. Then close the smoke box lid.
4. Turn dial to ROAST. Press WOODFIRE FLAVOR. Set temperature to 375°F, and set time to 15 minutes. Select START/STOP to begin preheating (preheating will take approx. 8–10 minutes).
5. When unit beeps to signify it has preheated and ADD FOOD is displayed, open hood and place mushroom caps in basket, stem-side down. Close hood to begin cooking.
6. With 9 minutes remaining, open hood and divide the marinara sauce, Mozzarella cheese and pepperoni evenly among the caps.
7. When cooking is complete, open hood, remove mushroom caps from basket, and serve.

Spinach and Carrot Balls

2 slices toasted bread
1 carrot, peeled and grated
1 package fresh spinach,
    blanched and chopped
½ onion, chopped
1 egg, beaten

½ tsp. garlic powder
1 tsp. minced garlic
1 tsp. salt
½ tsp. black pepper
1 tbsp. nutritional yeast
1 tbsp. flour

PREP: 10 minutes
PREHEAT: approx. 3 minutes
TOTAL COOK TIME: 10 minutes

1. In a food processor, pulse the toasted bread to form bread crumbs. Transfer into a shallow dish or bowl.
2. In a bowl, mix together all the other ingredients.
3. Use your hands to shape the mixture into small-sized balls. Roll the balls in the bread crumbs, ensuring to cover them well.
4. To install the grill grate, position it flat on top of the heating element and gently press down until it sits into place. Place Air Crisp Basket on grill grate, then close the hood.
5. Turn dial to AIR CRISP. Set temperature to 390°F, and set time to 10 minutes. Select START/STOP to begin preheating (preheating will take approx. 3 minutes).
6. When unit beeps to signify it has preheated and ADD FOOD is displayed, open hood and place the balls in basket. Close hood to begin cooking.
7. Several times during cooking, open hood and use silicone-tipped tongs to flip the balls.
8. When cooking is complete, open hood, remove the balls from basket, and serve.

Bistro Potato Wedges

1 pound (454 g) fingerling pota-
    toes, cut into wedges
1 tsp. extra-virgin olive oil
½ tsp. garlic powder
Salt and pepper, to taste
½ cup raw cashews, soaked in

    water overnight
½ tsp. ground turmeric
½ tsp. paprika
1 tbsp. nutritional yeast
1 tsp. fresh lemon juice
2 tbsps. to ¼ cup water

PREP: 10 minutes
PREHEAT: approx. 8-10 minutes
TOTAL COOK TIME: 20 minutes

1. In a bowl, toss together the potato wedges, olive oil, garlic powder, and salt and pepper, making sure to coat the potatoes well.
2. To install the grill grate, position it flat on top of the heating element and gently press down until it sits into place. Place Air Crisp Basket on grill grate, then close the hood.
3. While holding the smoke box lid open, use the pellet scoop to pour pellets into the smoke box until filled to the top. Then close the smoke box lid.
4. Turn dial to AIR CRISP. Press WOODFIRE FLAVOR. Set temperature to 390°F, and set time to 20 minutes. Select START/STOP to begin preheating (preheating will take approx. 8–10 minutes).
5. When unit beeps to signify it has preheated and ADD FOOD is displayed, open hood and place potatoes in basket. Close hood to begin cooking, shaking frequently during cooking.
6. In the meantime, prepare the cheese sauce. Pulse the cashews, turmeric, paprika, nutritional yeast, lemon juice, and water together in a food processor. Add more water to achieve your desired consistency.
7. With 3 minutes remaining, open hood and add the cheese sauce on top.
8. When cooking is complete, open hood, remove potatoes from basket, and serve.

Grilled Asparagus

SERVES: 4

PREP: 5 minutes
PREHEAT: approx. 15-19 minutes
TOTAL COOK TIME: 8 minutes

1 tbsp. olive oil
1 pound (454 g) fresh asparagus spears, trimmed
Salt and ground black pepper, to taste

1. Combine all the ingredients in a bowl.
2. To install the grill grate, position it flat on top of the heating element and gently press down until it sits into place, then close the hood.
3. While holding the smoke box lid open, use the pellet scoop to pour pellets into the smoke box until filled to the top. Then close the smoke box lid.
4. Turn dial to GRILL. Press WOODFIRE FLAVOR. Set temperature to HI, and set time to 8 minutes. Select START/STOP to begin preheating (preheating will take approx. 15–19 minutes).
5. When unit beeps to signify it has preheated and ADD FOOD is displayed, open hood and place the asparagus on grill grate, gently pressing them down to maximize grill marks. Close the hood and grill for 4 minutes. Then open hood, flip the asparagus, and grill for another 4 minutes.
6. When cooking is complete, open hood, remove the asparagus from grill. Serve hot.

Southwest Stuffed Peppers

SERVES: 6

PREP: 15 minutes
PREHEAT: approx. 8-10 minutes
TOTAL COOK TIME: 32 minutes

6 red or green bell peppers, seeded, ribs removed, and top ½-inch cut off and reserved
4 garlic cloves, minced
1 small white onion, diced
1 (10-ounce) can red or green enchilada sauce
2 (8.5-ounce) bags instant rice, cooked in microwave
½ tsp. chili powder
¼ tsp. ground cumin
½ cup canned black beans, rinsed and drained
½ cup frozen corn
½ cup vegetable stock
1 (8-ounce) bag shredded Colby Jack cheese, divided

1. Chop the ½-inch portions of reserved bell pepper and place in a large mixing bowl. Add the garlic, onion, cooked instant rice, enchilada sauce, chili powder, cumin, black beans, corn, vegetable stock, and half the cheese. Mix to combine well.
2. Spoon the mixture into the peppers, filling them up as full as possible. If necessary, lightly press the mixture down into the peppers to fit more in.
3. To install the grill grate, position it flat on top of the heating element and gently press down until it sits into place. Place Air Crisp Basket on grill grate, then close the hood.
4. While holding the smoke box lid open, use the pellet scoop to pour pellets into the smoke box until filled to the top. Then close the smoke box lid.
5. Turn dial to ROAST. Press WOODFIRE FLAVOR. Set temperature to 350°F, and set time to 32 minutes. Select START/STOP to begin preheating (preheating will take approx. 8–10 minutes).
6. When unit beeps to signify it has preheated and ADD FOOD is displayed, open hood and place the peppers, upright into basket. Close hood to begin cooking.
7. With 2 minutes remaining, open hood and sprinkle the remaining cheese over the top of the peppers.
8. When cooking is complete, open hood, remove the peppers from basket, and serve.

Spicy Hasselback Potatoes

SERVES: 4

4 russet potatoes, peeled
Salt and freshly ground black
  pepper, to taste

¼ cup grated Parmesan cheese
Cooking spray

PREP: 5 minutes
PREHEAT: approx. 8-10 minutes
TOTAL COOK TIME: 45 minutes

1. Make thin parallel cuts into each potato, ⅛-inch to ¼-inch apart, stopping at about ½ of the way through. The potato needs to stay intact along the bottom.
2. Spray the potatoes with cooking spray and use the hands or a silicone brush to completely coat the potatoes lightly in oil.
3. To install the grill grate, position it flat on top of the heating element and gently press down until it sits into place. Place Air Crisp Basket on grill grate, then close the hood.
4. While holding the smoke box lid open, use the pellet scoop to pour pellets into the smoke box until filled to the top. Then close the smoke box lid.
5. Turn dial to AIR CRISP. Press WOODFIRE FLAVOR. Set temperature to 390°F, and set time to 45 minutes. Select START/STOP to begin preheating (preheating will take approx. 8–10 minutes).
6. When unit beeps to signify it has preheated and ADD FOOD is displayed, open hood and place the potatoes in basket. Close hood to begin cooking.
7. With 20 minutes remaining, open hood and use silicone-tipped tongs to flip the potatoes.
8. When cooking is complete, open hood, remove the potatoes from basket. Sprinkle the potatoes with Parmesan cheese and serve.

Crispy Broccoli

SERVES: 1

4 egg yolks
¼ cup butter, melted
2 cups coconut flour
Salt and pepper, to taste
2 cups broccoli florets

PREP: 5 minutes
PREHEAT: approx. 3 minutes
TOTAL COOK TIME: 10 minutes

1. In a bowl, whisk the egg yolks and melted butter together. Throw in the coconut flour, salt and pepper, then stir again to combine well. Dip each broccoli floret into the mixture.
2. To install the grill grate, position it flat on top of the heating element and gently press down until it sits into place. Place Air Crisp Basket on grill grate, then close the hood.
3. Turn dial to AIR CRISP. Set temperature to 390°F, and set time to 10 minutes. Select START/STOP to begin preheating (preheating will take approx. 3 minutes).
4. When unit beeps to signify it has preheated and ADD FOOD is displayed, open hood and place the broccoli florets in basket. Close hood to begin cooking.
5. With 5 minutes remaining, open hood and use silicone-tipped tongs to flip the broccoli florets.
6. When cooking is complete, open hood, remove the broccoli florets from basket, and serve.

Golden Garlicky Mushrooms

SERVES: 4

PREP: 10 minutes
PREHEAT: approx. 8-10 minutes
TOTAL COOK TIME: 8 minutes

6 small mushrooms
1 tbsp. bread crumbs
1 tbsp. olive oil
1 ounce (28 g) onion, peeled and
diced

1 tsp. parsley
1 tsp. garlic purée
Salt and ground black pepper, to
taste

1. Combine the bread crumbs, oil, onion, parsley, salt, pepper and garlic in a bowl. Cut out the mushrooms' stalks and stuff each cap with the crumb mixture.
2. To install the grill grate, position it flat on top of the heating element and gently press down until it sits into place. Place Air Crisp Basket on grill grate, then close the hood.
3. While holding the smoke box lid open, use the pellet scoop to pour pellets into the smoke box until filled to the top. Then close the smoke box lid.
4. Turn dial to AIR CRISP. Press WOODFIRE FLAVOR. Set temperature to 390°F, and set time to 8 minutes. Select START/STOP to begin preheating (preheating will take approx. 8–10 minutes).
5. When unit beeps to signify it has preheated and ADD FOOD is displayed, open hood and place the mushroom in basket. Close hood to begin cooking.
6. When cooking is complete, open hood, remove the mushroom from basket, and serve.

CHAPTER 4: FISH AND SEAFOOD

Paprika Grilled Shrimp

SERVES: 2

1 pound tiger shrimp
2 tbsps. olive oil
½ tsp. smoked paprika
Salt, to taste

PREP: 10 minutes
PREHEAT: approx. 15-19 minutes
TOTAL COOK TIME: 5 minutes

1. Mix all the ingredients in a large bowl until well combined.
2. To install the grill grate, position it flat on top of the heating element and gently press down until it sits into place, then close the hood.
3. While holding the smoke box lid open, use the pellet scoop to pour pellets into the smoke box until filled to the top. Then close the smoke box lid.
4. Turn dial to GRILL. Press WOODFIRE FLAVOR. Set temperature to HI, and set time to 5 minutes. Select START/STOP to begin preheating (preheating will take approx. 15–19 minutes).
5. When unit beeps to signify it has preheated and ADD FOOD is displayed, open hood and place the shrimps on grill grate, gently pressing them down to maximize grill marks. Close the hood and grill for 3 minutes. Then open hood, flip the shrimps, and grill for another 2 minutes.
6. When cooking is complete, open hood, remove the shrimps from grill. Serve hot.

Glazed Fish Steak

SERVES: 4

1 pound haddock steak
1 garlic clove, minced
¼ tsp. fresh ginger, grated finely
½ cup low-sodium soy sauce
¼ cup fresh orange juice

2 tbsps. lime juice
½ cup cooking wine
¼ cup sugar
¼ tsp. red pepper flakes, crushed

PREP: 30 minutes
PREHEAT: approx. 15-19 minutes
TOTAL COOK TIME: 7 minutes

1. Put all the ingredients except haddock steak in a pan and bring to a boil.
2. Cook for about 4 minutes, stirring continuously and remove from the heat.
3. Put the haddock steak and half of the marinade in a resealable bag and shake well.
4. Refrigerate for about 1 hour and reserve the remaining marinade.
5. To install the grill grate, position it flat on top of the heating element and gently press down until it sits into place, then close the hood.
6. While holding the smoke box lid open, use the pellet scoop to pour pellets into the smoke box until filled to the top. Then close the smoke box lid.
7. Turn dial to GRILL. Press WOODFIRE FLAVOR. Set temperature to HI, and set time to 7 minutes. Select START/STOP to begin preheating (preheating will take approx. 15–19 minutes).
8. When unit beeps to signify it has preheated and ADD FOOD is displayed, open hood and place the haddock steaks on grill grate, gently pressing them down to maximize grill marks. Close the hood and grill for 4 minutes. Then open hood, flip the haddock steaks, and grill for another 3 minutes.
9. When cooking is complete, open hood, remove the haddock steaks from grill. Coat with the remaining glaze and serve hot.

Super-Simple Grilled Scallops

SERVES: 2

PREP: 10 minutes
PREHEAT: approx. 15-19 minutes
TOTAL COOK TIME: 6 minutes

¾ pound sea scallops
1 tbsp. clarified butter
½ tbsp. fresh thyme, minced
Salt and black pepper, to taste

1. Mix all the ingredients in a bowl and toss to coat well.
2. To install the grill grate, position it flat on top of the heating element and gently press down until it sits into place, then close the hood.
3. While holding the smoke box lid open, use the pellet scoop to pour pellets into the smoke box until filled to the top. Then close the smoke box lid.
4. Turn dial to GRILL. Press WOODFIRE FLAVOR. Set temperature to HI, and set time to 6 minutes. Select START/STOP to begin preheating (preheating will take approx. 15–19 minutes).
5. When unit beeps to signify it has preheated and ADD FOOD is displayed, open hood and place scallops on grill grate, gently pressing them down to maximize grill marks. Close the hood and grill for 3 minutes. Then open hood, flip scallops, and grill for another 3 minutes.
6. When cooking is complete, open hood, remove scallops from grill. Serve hot.

Herbed Haddock

SERVES: 2

PREP: 10 minutes
PREHEAT: approx. 15-19 minutes
TOTAL COOK TIME: 6 minutes

2 (6-ounce) haddock fillets
2 tbsps. pine nuts
3 tbsps. fresh basil, chopped
1 tbsp. Parmesan cheese, grated
½ cup extra-virgin olive oil
Salt and black pepper, to taste

1. Coat the haddock fillets evenly with olive oil and season with salt and black pepper.
2. To install the grill grate, position it flat on top of the heating element and gently press down until it sits into place, then close the hood.
3. While holding the smoke box lid open, use the pellet scoop to pour pellets into the smoke box until filled to the top. Then close the smoke box lid.
4. Turn dial to GRILL. Press WOODFIRE FLAVOR. Set temperature to HI, and set time to 6 minutes. Select START/STOP to begin preheating (preheating will take approx. 15–19 minutes).
5. Meanwhile, put remaining ingredients in a food processor and pulse until smooth.
6. When unit beeps to signify it has preheated and ADD FOOD is displayed, open hood and place the haddock fillets on grill grate, gently pressing them down to maximize grill marks. Close the hood and grill for 3 minutes. Then open hood, flip the haddock fillets, and grill for another 3 minutes.
7. When cooking is complete, open hood, remove the haddock fillets from grill. Top this cheese sauce over the haddock fillets and serve hot.

Miso-Glazed Cod and Grilled Bok Choy

SERVES: 4

4 (6-ounce) cod fillets
¼ cup miso
3 tbsps. brown sugar
1 tsp. sesame oil, divided
1 tbsp. white wine or mirin

2 tbsps. soy sauce
¼ tsp. red pepper flakes
1 pound baby bok choy, halved
 lengthwise

PREP: 5 minutes
PREHEAT: approx. 15-19 minutes
TOTAL COOK TIME: 18 minutes

1. Place the cod, miso, brown sugar, ¾ tsp. of sesame oil, and white wine in a large resealable plastic bag or container. Move the fillets around to coat evenly with the marinade. Refrigerate for 30 minutes.
2. To install the grill grate, position it flat on top of the heating element and gently press down until it sits into place, then close the hood.
3. While holding the smoke box lid open, use the pellet scoop to pour pellets into the smoke box until filled to the top. Then close the smoke box lid.
4. Turn dial to GRILL. Press WOODFIRE FLAVOR. Set temperature to HI, and set time to 18 minutes. Select START/STOP to begin preheating (preheating will take approx. 15–19 minutes).
5. Meanwhile, whisk together the remaining ¼ tsp. of sesame oil, soy sauce, and red pepper flakes in a small bowl. Brush the bok choy halves with the soy sauce mixture on all sides.
6. When unit beeps to signify it has preheated and ADD FOOD is displayed, open hood and place cod fillets on grill grate, gently pressing them down to maximize grill marks. Close the hood and grill for 4 minutes. Then open hood, flip cod fillets, and grill for another 4 minutes.
7. Remove the cod from the grill and set aside on a cutting board to rest. Tent with aluminum foil to keep warm. Place the bok choy on the grill and close the hood to continue cooking, tossing frequently during cooking.
8. When cooking is complete, open hood, remove the bok choy from grill. Plate the bok choy with the cod, and serve.

Spicy Sriracha-Glazed Salmon

SERVES: 4

1 cup sriracha
Juice of 2 lemons
¼ cup honey
4 (6-ounce) skinless salmon fillets
Chives, chopped, for garnish

PREP: 10 minutes
PREHEAT: approx. 15-19 minutes
TOTAL COOK TIME: 8 minutes

1. Place the sriracha, lemon juice, and honey in a large resealable plastic bag or container. Add the salmon fillets and coat evenly. Refrigerate for 30 minutes.
2. To install the grill grate, position it flat on top of the heating element and gently press down until it sits into place, then close the hood.
3. While holding the smoke box lid open, use the pellet scoop to pour pellets into the smoke box until filled to the top. Then close the smoke box lid.
4. Turn dial to GRILL. Press WOODFIRE FLAVOR. Set temperature to HI, and set time to 8 minutes. Select START/STOP to begin preheating (preheating will take approx. 15–19 minutes).
5. When unit beeps to signify it has preheated and ADD FOOD is displayed, open hood and place fillets on grill grate, gently pressing them down to maximize grill marks. Close the hood and grill for 4 minutes. Then open hood, flip fillets, and grill for another 4 minutes.
6. When cooking is complete, open hood, remove fillets from grill. Plate, and garnish with the chives.

Maple Grilled Salmon

SERVES: 2

PREP: 10 minutes
PREHEAT: approx. 15-19 minutes
TOTAL COOK TIME: 7 minutes

2 (6-ounces) salmon fillets
Salt, to taste
2 tbsps. maple syrup

1. Coat the salmon fillets evenly with maple syrup and season with salt.
2. To install the grill grate, position it flat on top of the heating element and gently press down until it sits into place, then close the hood.
3. While holding the smoke box lid open, use the pellet scoop to pour pellets into the smoke box until filled to the top. Then close the smoke box lid.
4. Turn dial to GRILL. Press WOODFIRE FLAVOR. Set temperature to HI, and set time to 7 minutes. Select START/STOP to begin preheating (preheating will take approx. 15–19 minutes).
5. When unit beeps to signify it has preheated and ADD FOOD is displayed, open hood and place the salmon fillets on grill grate, gently pressing them down to maximize grill marks. Close the hood and grill for 4 minutes. Then open the hood, flip the salmon fillets, and grill for another 3 minutes.
6. When cooking is complete, open hood, remove the salmon fillets from grill. Serve hot.

Classic Crispy Fish Sticks

SERVES: 4

PREP: 10 minutes
PREHEAT: approx. 3 minutes
TOTAL COOK TIME: 10 minutes

1 pound cod fillets
¼ cup all-purpose flour
1 large egg
1 tsp. Dijon mustard
½ cup bread crumbs
1 tbsp. dried parsley
1 tsp. paprika
½ tsp. freshly ground black pepper
Nonstick cooking spray

1. Place the flour on a plate. In a medium shallow bowl, whisk together the egg and Dijon mustard. In a separate medium shallow bowl, combine the bread crumbs, dried parsley, paprika, and black pepper.
2. Cut the fish fillets into ¾- to 1-inch-wide strips.
3. One at a time, dredge the cod strips in the flour, shaking off any excess, then coat them in the egg mixture. Finally, dredge them in the bread crumb mixture, and coat on all sides.
4. To install the grill grate, position it flat on top of the heating element and gently press down until it sits into place. Place Air Crisp Basket on grill grate, then close the hood.
5. Turn dial to AIR CRISP. Set temperature to 390°F, and set time to 10 minutes. Select START/STOP to begin preheating (preheating will take approx. 3 minutes).
6. When unit beeps to signify it has preheated and ADD FOOD is displayed, open hood. Spray the basket lightly with cooking spray and place the cod strips in basket. Close hood to begin cooking.
7. With 5 minutes remaining, open hood and use silicone-tipped tongs to flip the cod strips.
8. When cooking is complete, open hood, remove the cod strips from basket, and serve.

Crab Cakes with Cajun Aioli

SERVES: 4

1 egg
½ cup mayonnaise, plus 3 tbsps.
Juice of ½ lemon
1 tbsp. minced scallions (green parts only)
1 tsp. Old Bay seasoning
8 ounces lump crabmeat
⅓ cup bread crumbs

Nonstick cooking spray
½ tsp. cayenne pepper
¼ tsp. paprika
¼ tsp. garlic powder
¼ tsp. chili powder
¼ tsp. onion powder
¼ tsp. freshly ground black pepper
⅛ tsp. ground nutmeg

PREP: 10 minutes
PREHEAT: approx. 8-10 minutes
TOTAL COOK TIME: 10 minutes

1. In a medium bowl, whisk together the egg, 3 tbsps. of mayonnaise, lemon juice, scallions, and Old Bay seasoning. Gently stir in the crabmeat, making sure not to break up the meat into small pieces. Add the bread crumbs, and gradually mix them in. Form the mixture into four patties.
2. To install the grill grate, position it flat on top of the heating element and gently press down until it sits into place. Place Air Crisp Basket on grill grate, then close the hood.
3. While holding the smoke box lid open, use the pellet scoop to pour pellets into the smoke box until filled to the top. Then close the smoke box lid.
4. Turn dial to AIR CRISP. Press WOODFIRE FLAVOR. Set temperature to 375°F, and set time to 10 minutes. Select START/STOP to begin preheating (preheating will take approx. 8–10 minutes).
5. When unit beeps to signify it has preheated and ADD FOOD is displayed, open hood. Spray the basket lightly with cooking spray and place crab cakes in basket. Close hood to begin cooking.
6. With 5 minutes remaining, open hood and use silicone-tipped tongs to flip the crab cakes.
7. Meanwhile, mix the remaining ½ cup of mayonnaise, cayenne pepper, paprika, garlic powder, chili powder, onion powder, black pepper, and nutmeg in a small bowl until fully combined.
8. When cooking is complete, open hood, remove crab cakes from basket. Serve the crab cakes with the Cajun aioli spooned on top.

Juicy Salmon and Asparagus Parcels

SERVES: 2

2 salmon fillets
4 asparagus stalks
¼ cup champagne
Salt and black pepper, to taste
¼ cup white sauce
1 tsp. olive oil

PREP: 5 minutes
PREHEAT: approx. 8-10 minutes
TOTAL COOK TIME: 13 minutes

1. Mix all the ingredients in a bowl and divide this mixture evenly over 2 foil papers.
2. To install the grill grate, position it flat on top of the heating element and gently press down until it sits into place. Place Air Crisp Basket on grill grate, then close the hood.
3. While holding the smoke box lid open, use the pellet scoop to pour pellets into the smoke box until filled to the top. Then close the smoke box lid.
4. Turn dial to ROAST. Press WOODFIRE FLAVOR. Set temperature to 355°F, and set time to 13 minutes. Select START/STOP to begin preheating (preheating will take approx. 8–10 minutes).
5. When unit beeps to signify it has preheated and ADD FOOD is displayed, open hood and place the foil papers in basket. Close hood to begin cooking.
6. When cooking is complete, open hood, remove the foil papers from basket. Serve hot.

Spicy Cod

PREP: 10 minutes
PREHEAT: approx. 15-19 minutes
TOTAL COOK TIME: 6 minutes

2 (6-ounces) (1½-inch thick) cod fillets
1 tsp. smoked paprika
1 tsp. cayenne pepper
1 tsp. onion powder
1 tsp. garlic powder
Salt and ground black pepper, as required
2 tsps. olive oil

1. Drizzle the cod fillets with olive oil and rub with the all the spices.
2. To install the grill grate, position it flat on top of the heating element and gently press down until it sits into place, then close the hood.
3. While holding the smoke box lid open, use the pellet scoop to pour pellets into the smoke box until filled to the top. Then close the smoke box lid.
4. Turn dial to GRILL. Press WOODFIRE FLAVOR. Set temperature to HI, and set time to 6 minutes. Select START/STOP to begin pre-heating (preheating will take approx. 15–19 minutes).
5. When unit beeps to signify it has preheated and ADD FOOD is displayed, open hood and place the cod fillets on grill grate, gently pressing them down to maximize grill marks. Close the hood and grill for 3 minutes. Then open hood, flip the cod fillets, and grill for another 3 minutes.
6. When cooking is complete, open hood, remove the cod fillets from grill. Serve hot.

Grilled Swordfish in Caper Sauce

PREP: 5 minutes
PREHEAT: approx. 15-19 minutes
TOTAL COOK TIME: 8 minutes

1 tbsp. freshly squeezed lemon juice
1 tbsp. extra-virgin olive oil
Sea salt
Freshly ground black pepper
4 fresh (8-ounce) swordfish steaks,
about 1-inch thick
4 tbsps. unsalted butter
1 lemon, sliced crosswise into 8 slices
2 tbsps. capers, drained

1. In a large shallow bowl, whisk together the lemon juice and oil. Season the swordfish steaks with salt and pepper on each side, and place them in the oil mixture. Turn to coat both sides. Refrigerate for 15 minutes.
2. To install the grill grate, position it flat on top of the heating element and gently press down until it sits into place, then close the hood.
3. While holding the smoke box lid open, use the pellet scoop to pour pellets into the smoke box until filled to the top. Then close the smoke box lid.
4. Turn dial to GRILL. Press WOODFIRE FLAVOR. Set temperature to HI, and set time to 8 minutes. Select START/STOP to begin preheating (preheating will take approx. 15–19 minutes).
5. Meanwhile, melt the butter in a small saucepan over medium heat. Stir and cook for about 3 minutes, until the butter has slightly browned. Add the lemon slices and capers to the pan, and cook for 1 minute. Turn off the heat.
6. When unit beeps to signify it has preheated and ADD FOOD is displayed, open hood and place the steaks on grill grate, gently pressing them down to maximize grill marks. Close the hood and grill for 4 minutes. Then open hood, flip the steaks, and grill for another 4 minutes.
7. When cooking is complete, open hood, transfer the steaks to a cutting board. Slice the steaks into thick strips. Plate, pour the caper sauce over the top, and serve immediately.

Coconut Shrimp

SERVES: 4

½ cup all-purpose flour
2 tsps. freshly ground black pepper
½ tsp. sea salt
2 large eggs
¾ cup unsweetened coconut flakes

¼ cup panko bread crumbs
24 peeled, deveined shrimp
Nonstick cooking spray
Sweet chili sauce, for serving

PREP: 15 minutes
PREHEAT: approx. 3 minutes
TOTAL COOK TIME: 8 minutes

1. In a medium shallow bowl, mix together the flour, black pepper, and salt. In a second medium shallow bowl, whisk the eggs. In a third, combine the coconut flakes and bread crumbs.
2. Dredge each shrimp in the flour mixture, then in the egg. Press each shrimp into the coconut mixture on both sides, leaving the tail uncoated.
3. To install the grill grate, position it flat on top of the heating element and gently press down until it sits into place. Place Air Crisp Basket on grill grate, then close the hood.
4. Turn dial to AIR CRISP. Set temperature to 390°F, and set time to 8 minutes. Select START/STOP to begin preheating (preheating will take approx. 3 minutes).
5. When unit beeps to signify it has preheated and ADD FOOD is displayed, open hood and place the shrimp in basket. Close hood to begin cooking.
6. With 4 minutes remaining, open hood and use silicone-tipped tongs to flip the shrimp.
7. When cooking is complete, open hood, remove the shrimp from basket, and serve with sweet chili sauce.

Lemon-Garlic Shrimp Caesar Salad

SERVES: 4

1 pound fresh jumbo shrimps
Juice of ½ lemon
3 garlic cloves, minced
Sea salt
Freshly ground black pepper

2 heads romaine lettuce, chopped
½ cup grated Parmesan cheese
¾ cup Caesar dressing

PREP: 10 minutes
PREHEAT: approx. 15-19 minutes
TOTAL COOK TIME: 5 minutes

1. In a large bowl, toss the shrimps with the lemon juice, garlic, salt, and pepper. Let marinate for 5 minutes.
2. To install the grill grate, position it flat on top of the heating element and gently press down until it sits into place, then close the hood.
3. While holding the smoke box lid open, use the pellet scoop to pour pellets into the smoke box until filled to the top. Then close the smoke box lid.
4. Turn dial to GRILL. Press WOODFIRE FLAVOR. Set temperature to HI, and set time to 5 minutes. Select START/STOP to begin preheating (preheating will take approx. 15–19 minutes).
5. Meanwhile, toss the romaine lettuce with the Caesar dressing, then divide evenly among four plates or bowls.
6. When unit beeps to signify it has preheated and ADD FOOD is displayed, open hood and place the shrimps on grill grate, gently pressing them down to maximize grill marks. Close the hood and grill for 3 minutes. Then open hood, flip the shrimps, and grill for another 2 minutes.
7. When cooking is complete, open hood, remove the shrimps from grill. Place the shrimps on top of each salad. Sprinkle with the Parmesan cheese and serve.

Cajun Spiced Salmon

SERVES: 2

PREP: 10 minutes
PREHEAT: approx. 15-19 minutes
TOTAL COOK TIME: 8 minutes

2 (7-ounces) (¾-inch thick) salmon fillets
1 tbsp. Cajun seasoning
½ tsp. coconut sugar
1 tbsp. fresh lemon juice

1. Season the salmon evenly with Cajun seasoning and coconut sugar.
2. To install the grill grate, position it flat on top of the heating element and gently press down until it sits into place, then close the hood.
3. While holding the smoke box lid open, use the pellet scoop to pour pellets into the smoke box until filled to the top. Then close the smoke box lid.
4. Turn dial to GRILL. Press WOODFIRE FLAVOR. Set temperature to HI, and set time to 8 minutes. Select START/STOP to begin pre-heating (preheating will take approx. 15–19 minutes).
5. When unit beeps to signify it has preheated and ADD FOOD is displayed, open hood and place the salmon fillets on grill grate, gently pressing them down to maximize grill marks. Close the hood and grill for 4 minutes. Then open hood, flip the salmon fillets, and grill for another 4 minutes.
6. When cooking is complete, open hood, remove the salmon fillets from grill. Drizzle with the lemon juice and serve hot.

Seared Tuna Salad

SERVES: 4

PREP: 10 minutes
PREHEAT: approx. 15-19 minutes
TOTAL COOK TIME: 8 minutes

2 tbsps. rice wine vinegar
¼ tsp. sea salt, plus additional for seasoning
½ tsp. freshly ground black pepper, plus additional for seasoning
6 tbsps. extra-virgin olive oil
1½ pounds ahi tuna, cut into four strips
2 tbsps. sesame oil
1 (10-ounce) bag baby greens
½ English cucumber, sliced

1. In a small bowl, whisk together the rice vinegar, ¼ tsp. of salt, and ½ tsp. of pepper. Slowly pour in the oil while whisking, until the vinaigrette is fully combined.
2. Season the tuna with salt and pepper, and drizzle with the sesame oil.
3. To install the grill grate, position it flat on top of the heating element and gently press down until it sits into place, then close the hood.
4. While holding the smoke box lid open, use the pellet scoop to pour pellets into the smoke box until filled to the top. Then close the smoke box lid.
5. Turn dial to GRILL. Press WOODFIRE FLAVOR. Set temperature to HI, and set time to 8 minutes. Select START/STOP to begin preheating (preheating will take approx. 15–19 minutes).
6. When unit beeps to signify it has preheated and ADD FOOD is displayed, open hood and place the tuna strips on grill grate, gently pressing them down to maximize grill marks. Close the hood and grill for 4 minutes. Then open hood, flip the tuna strips, and grill for another 4 minutes.
7. While the tuna cooks, divide the baby greens and cucumber slices evenly among four plates or bowls.
8. When cooking is complete, open hood, remove the tuna the tuna strips from grill. Top each salad with one tuna strip. Drizzle the vinaigrette over the top, and serve immediately.

CHAPTER 5: BEEF

Beef Jerky

SERVES: 3

1 pound bottom round beef, cut into thin strips
½ cup dark brown sugar
½ cup soy sauce
¼ cup Worcestershire sauce
1 tbsp. chili pepper sauce

1 tbsp. hickory liquid smoke
1 tsp. garlic powder
1 tsp. onion powder
1 tsp. cayenne pepper
½ tsp. smoked paprika
½ tsp. ground black pepper

PREP: 20 minutes
TOTAL COOK TIME: 5-6 hours

1. Mix the brown sugar, all sauces, liquid smoke, and spices in a bowl.
2. Coat the beef strips with this marinade generously and marinate overnight.
3. To install the grill grate, position it flat on top of the heating element and gently press down until it sits into place.
4. Remove the beef from the marinade and discard excess liquid. Place the beef in a flat single layer in the Air Crisp Basket. Then place the basket on the grill grate and close the hood.
5. While holding the smoke box lid open, use the pellet scoop to pour pellets into the smoke box until filled to the top. Then close the smoke box lid.
6. Turn dial to DEHYDRATE. Press WOODFIRE FLAVOR. Set temperature to 150°F, and set time to 6 hours. Select START/STOP to begin preheating (preheating is not needed).
7. Begin to check the beef jerky after 5 hours. If a crispier output is desired, continue to cook.
8. When cooking is complete, open hood and remove basket with beef jerky. Beef jerky can be stored in an air-tight container for up to 1 week.

Grilled Jalapeño Popper Burgers

SERVES: 4

2 jalapeño peppers, seeded, stemmed, and minced
½ cup shredded Cheddar cheese
4 ounces cream cheese, at room temperature
4 slices bacon, cooked and crumbled
2 pounds ground beef

½ tsp. chili powder
¼ tsp. paprika
¼ tsp. freshly ground black pepper
4 hamburger buns
4 slices pepper Jack cheese
Lettuce, sliced tomato, and sliced red onion, for topping (optional)

PREP: 5 minutes
PREHEAT: approx. 15-19 minutes
TOTAL COOK TIME: 8 minutes

1. In a medium bowl, combine the peppers, Cheddar cheese, cream cheese, and bacon until well combined.
2. Form the ground beef into 8 (¼-inch-thick) patties. Spoon some of the filling mixture onto four of the patties, then place a second patty on top of each to make four burgers. Use your fingers to pinch the edges of the patties together to seal in the filling. Reshape the patties with your hands as needed.
3. Combine the chili powder, paprika, and pepper in a small bowl. Sprinkle the mixture onto both sides of the burgers.
4. To install the grill grate, position it flat on top of the heating element and gently press down until it sits into place, then close the hood.
5. While holding the smoke box lid open, use the pellet scoop to pour pellets into the smoke box until filled to the top. Then close the smoke box lid.
6. Turn dial to GRILL. Press WOODFIRE FLAVOR. Set temperature to HI, and set time to 8 minutes. Select START/STOP to begin preheating (preheating will take approx. 15–19 minutes).
7. When unit beeps to signify it has preheated and ADD FOOD is displayed, open hood and place the burgers on grill grate, gently pressing them down to maximize grill marks. Close the hood and grill for 4 minutes. Then open hood, flip the burgers, and grill for another 4 minutes.
8. Cooking is complete when the internal temperature of the beef reaches at least 145°F on a food thermometer.
9. When cooking is complete, open hood, remove the burgers from grill. Place the burgers on the hamburger buns and top with pepper Jack cheese. Add lettuce, tomato, and red onion, if desired.

Spicy Smoked Beef

SERVES: 8

PREP: 10 minutes
TOTAL COOK TIME: 5 hours

3 pounds roast beef, at room temperature
3 tbsps. extra-virgin olive oil
1 tsp. sea salt flakes
1 tbsp. black pepper, preferably freshly ground
1 tbsp. smoked paprika
A few dashes of liquid smoke
2 jalapeño peppers, thinly sliced

1. Pat the roast dry using kitchen towels. Rub with extra-virgin olive oil and all seasonings along with liquid smoke.
2. To install the grill grate, position it flat on top of the heating element and gently press down until it sits into place.
3. Place the beef on the grill grate, then close the hood.
4. While holding the smoke box lid open, use the pellet scoop to pour pellets into the smoke box until filled to the top. Then close the smoke box lid.
5. Turn dial to SMOKER and set temperature to 250°F, and set time to 5 hours. Select START/ STOP to begin cooking (preheating is not needed).
6. Cooking is complete when an instant-read thermometer reads 203°F. When cooking is complete, open hood, remove the beef from grill, and let rest for 30 minutes. Then shred the beef and serve sprinkled with sliced jalapeños. Bon appétit!

Grilled Steak Salad with Blue Cheese Dressing

SERVES: 4

PREP: 5 minutes
PREHEAT: approx. 15-19 minutes
TOTAL COOK TIME: 10 minutes

4 (8-ounce) skirt steaks
Sea salt
Freshly ground black pepper
6 cups chopped romaine lettuce
¾ cup cherry tomatoes, halved

¼ cup blue cheese, crumbled
1 cup croutons
2 avocados, peeled and sliced
1 cup blue cheese dressing

1. Season the steaks on both sides with the salt and pepper.
2. To install the grill grate, position it flat on top of the heating element and gently press down until it sits into place, then close the hood.
3. While holding the smoke box lid open, use the pellet scoop to pour pellets into the smoke box until filled to the top. Then close the smoke box lid.
4. Turn dial to GRILL. Press WOODFIRE FLAVOR. Set temperature to HI, and set time to 10 minutes. Select START/STOP to begin preheating (preheating will take approx. 15–19 minutes).
5. When unit beeps to signify it has preheated and ADD FOOD is displayed, open hood and place the steaks on grill grate, gently pressing them down to maximize grill marks. Close the hood and grill for 5 minutes. Then open hood, flip the steaks, and grill for another 5 minutes.
6. Meanwhile, assemble the salad by tossing together the lettuce, tomatoes, blue cheese crumbles, and croutons. Top with the avocado slices.
7. When cooking is complete, open hood, remove the steaks from grill. Slice the steaks into thin strips, and place on top of the salad. Drizzle with the blue cheese dressing and serve.

Grilled New York Strip Steak

1 (9½-ounces) New York strip steak
1 tsp. olive oil
Crushed red pepper flakes, to taste
Salt and black pepper, to taste

PREP: 10 minutes
PREHEAT: approx. 15-19 minutes
TOTAL COOK TIME: 8 minutes

1. Rub the steak generously with red pepper flakes, salt and black pepper and coat with olive oil.
2. To install the grill grate, position it flat on top of the heating element and gently press down until it sits into place, then close the hood.
3. While holding the smoke box lid open, use the pellet scoop to pour pellets into the smoke box until filled to the top. Then close the smoke box lid.
4. Turn dial to GRILL. Press WOODFIRE FLAVOR. Set temperature to HI, and set time to 8 minutes. Select START/STOP to begin preheating (preheating will take approx. 15–19 minutes).
5. When unit beeps to signify it has preheated and ADD FOOD is displayed, open hood and place the steak on grill grate, gently pressing it down to maximize grill marks. Close the hood and grill for 4 minutes. Then open hood, flip the steak, and grill for another 4 minutes.
6. When cooking is complete, open hood, remove the steak from grill. Cut into desired size slices to serve.

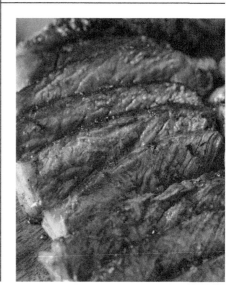

Beef Steak Fingers

4 small beef cube steaks
Salt and ground black pepper, to taste
½ cup whole wheat flour
Cooking spray

PREP: 5 minutes
PREHEAT: approx. 8-10 minutes
TOTAL COOK TIME: 8 minutes

1. Cut cube steaks into 1-inch-wide strips. Sprinkle lightly with salt and pepper to taste. Roll in flour to coat all sides.
2. To install the grill grate, position it flat on top of the heating element and gently press down until it sits into place. Place Air Crisp Basket on grill grate, then close the hood.
3. While holding the smoke box lid open, use the pellet scoop to pour pellets into the smoke box until filled to the top. Then close the smoke box lid.
4. Turn dial to AIR CRISP. Press WOODFIRE FLAVOR. Set temperature to 390°F, and set time to 8 minutes. Select START/STOP to begin preheating (preheating will take approx. 8–10 minutes).
5. When unit beeps to signify it has preheated and ADD FOOD is displayed, open hood. Spritz the basket with cooking spray and place the steak strips in basket. Close hood to begin cooking, shaking frequently during cooking.
6. Test with fork for doneness. Steak fingers should be crispy outside with no red juices inside.
7. When cooking is complete, open hood, remove the steak fingers from basket, and serve.

Filet Mignon with Pineapple Salsa

PREP: 15 minutes
PREHEAT: approx. 15-19 minutes
TOTAL COOK TIME: 16 minutes

4 (6- to 8-ounce) filet mignon steaks
1 tbsp. canola oil, divided
Sea salt
Freshly ground black pepper
½ medium pineapple, cored and diced
1 medium red onion, diced
1 jalapeño pepper, seeded, stemmed, and diced
1 tbsp. freshly squeezed lime juice
¼ cup chopped fresh cilantro leaves
Chili powder
Ground coriander

1. Rub each filet on all sides with ½ tbsp. of the oil, then season with the salt and pepper.
2. To install the grill grate, position it flat on top of the heating element and gently press down until it sits into place, then close the hood.
3. While holding the smoke box lid open, use the pellet scoop to pour pellets into the smoke box until filled to the top. Then close the smoke box lid.
4. Turn dial to GRILL. Press WOODFIRE FLAVOR. Set temperature to HI, and set time to 16 minutes. Select START/STOP to begin preheating (preheating will take approx. 15–19 minutes).
5. When unit beeps to signify it has preheated and ADD FOOD is displayed, open hood and place the filets on grill grate, gently pressing them down to maximize grill marks. Close the hood and grill for 8 minutes. Then open hood, flip the filets, and grill for another 8 minutes.
6. When cooking is complete, open hood, remove the filets from grill. Let rest for a total of 10 minutes; this allows the natural juices to redistribute into the steak.
7. While the filets rest, in a medium bowl, combine the pineapple, onion, and jalapeño. Stir in the lime juice and cilantro, then season to taste with the chili powder and coriander.
8. Plate the filets, and pile the salsa on top of each before serving.

Chili-Rubbed Flank Steak

PREP: 10 minutes
PREHEAT: approx. 15-19 minutes
TOTAL COOK TIME: 10 minutes

1 tbsp. chili powder
1 tsp. dried oregano
2 tsps. ground cumin
1 tsp. sea salt
¼ tsp. freshly ground black pepper
2 (8-ounce) flank steaks

1. In a small bowl, mix together the chili powder, oregano, cumin, salt, and pepper. Use your hands to rub the spice mixture on all sides of the steaks.
2. To install the grill grate, position it flat on top of the heating element and gently press down until it sits into place, then close the hood.
3. While holding the smoke box lid open, use the pellet scoop to pour pellets into the smoke box until filled to the top. Then close the smoke box lid.
4. Turn dial to GRILL. Press WOODFIRE FLAVOR. Set temperature to HI, and set time to 10 minutes. Select START/STOP to begin preheating (preheating will take approx. 15–19 minutes).
5. When unit beeps to signify it has preheated and ADD FOOD is displayed, open hood and place the steaks on grill grate, gently pressing them down to maximize grill marks. Close the hood and grill for 5 minutes. Then open hood, flip the steaks, and grill for another 5 minutes.
6. When cooking is complete, open hood, remove the steaks from grill. Transfer them to a cutting board. Let rest for 5 minutes before slicing and serving.

Bacon Wrapped Filet Mignon

SERVES: 2

2 bacon slices
2 (6-ounces) filet mignon steaks
Salt and black pepper, to taste
1 tsp. avocado oil
½ cup BBQ Sauce for serving

PREP: 15 minutes
PREHEAT: approx. 15-19 minutes
TOTAL COOK TIME: 16 minutes

1. Wrap each mignon steak with 1 bacon slice and secure with a toothpick.
2. Season the steak generously with salt and black pepper and coat with avocado oil.
3. To install the grill grate, position it flat on top of the heating element and gently press down until it sits into place, then close the hood.
4. While holding the smoke box lid open, use the pellet scoop to pour pellets into the smoke box until filled to the top. Then close the smoke box lid.
5. Turn dial to GRILL. Press WOODFIRE FLAVOR. Set temperature to HI, and set time to 16 minutes. Select START/STOP to begin preheating (preheating will take approx. 15–19 minutes).
6. When unit beeps to signify it has preheated and ADD FOOD is displayed, open hood and place the steaks on grill grate, gently pressing them down to maximize grill marks. Close the hood and grill for 8 minutes. Then open hood, flip the steaks, and grill for another 8 minutes.
7. When cooking is complete, open hood, remove the steaks from grill. Cut them into desired size slices and serve with the BBQ sauce.

Provolone Stuffed Beef and Pork Meatballs

SERVES: 4-6

1 tbsp. olive oil
1 small onion, finely chopped
1 to 2 cloves garlic, minced
¾ pound (340 g) ground beef
¾ pound (340 g) ground pork
¾ cup bread crumbs
¼ cup grated Parmesan cheese
¼ cup finely chopped fresh parsley
½ tsp. dried oregano
1½ tsps. salt
Freshly ground black pepper, to taste
2 eggs, lightly beaten
5 ounces (142 g) sharp or aged provolone cheese, cut into 1-inch cubes

PREP: 15 minutes
PREHEAT: approx. 15-19 minutes
TOTAL COOK TIME: 14 minutes

1. Preheat a skillet over medium-high heat. Add the oil and cook the onion and garlic until tender, but not browned.
2. Transfer the onion and garlic to a large bowl and add the beef, pork, bread crumbs, Parmesan cheese, parsley, oregano, salt, pepper and eggs. Mix well until all the ingredients are combined. Divide the mixture into 12 evenly sized balls. Make one meatball at a time, by pressing a hole in the meatball mixture with the finger and pushing a piece of provolone cheese into the hole. Mold the meat back into a ball, enclosing the cheese.
3. To install the grill grate, position it flat on top of the heating element and gently press down until it sits into place, then close the hood.
4. While holding the smoke box lid open, use the pellet scoop to pour pellets into the smoke box until filled to the top. Then close the smoke box lid.
5. Turn dial to GRILL. Press WOODFIRE FLAVOR. Set temperature to HI, and set time to 14 minutes. Select START/STOP to begin preheating (preheating will take approx. 15–19 minutes).
6. When unit beeps to signify it has preheated and ADD FOOD is displayed, open hood and place the meatballs on grill grate, gently pressing them down to maximize grill marks. Close the hood and grill for 7 minutes. Then open hood, flip the meatballs, and grill for another 7 minutes.
7. When cooking is complete, open hood, remove the meatballs from grill. Serve warm.

Jerk Smoked Beef

PREP: 10 minutes
TOTAL COOK TIME: 4 hours

2 pounds beef roast
1 tbsp. olive oil
½ cup Jamaican Jerk Spice Blend

1. Rub the roast generously with the Spice Blend and coat with olive oil.
2. To install the grill grate, position it flat on top of the heating element and gently press down until it sits into place.
3. Place the roast on the grill grate, then close the hood.
4. While holding the smoke box lid open, use the pellet scoop to pour pellets into the smoke box until filled to the top. Then close the smoke box lid.
5. Turn dial to SMOKER and set temperature to 250°F, and set time to 4 hours. Select START/ STOP to begin cooking (preheating is not needed).
6. Cooking is complete when an instant-read thermometer reads 203°F. When cooking is complete, open hood, remove the roast from grill, and let rest for 30 minutes. Cut into desired size slices and serve with your desired sauce.

Jamaican Jerk Spice Blend: 1 tbsp. garlic powder, 1 tbsp. onion powder, 1 tbsp. brown sugar, 1 tbsp. dried parsley, 2 tsps. cayenne pepper, 1 tsp. ground cinnamon, 1 tsp. kosher salt, ½ tsp. black pepper, ½ tsp. ground allspice, ½ tsp. ground clove, ½ tsp. red pepper flakes, ½ tsp. chili powder, ½ tsp. paprika, ½ tsp. ground nutmeg

Crispy Sirloin Steak

PREP: 15 minutes
PREHEAT: approx. 8-10 minutes
TOTAL COOK TIME: 12 minutes

1 cup white flour
2 eggs
1 cup panko breadcrumbs
2 (6-ounces) sirloin steaks, pounded

1 tsp. garlic powder
1 tsp. onion powder
Salt and black pepper, to taste

1. Place the flour in a shallow bowl and whisk eggs in a second dish.
2. Mix the panko breadcrumbs and spices in a third bowl.
3. Rub the steaks with flour, dip into the eggs and coat with breadcrumb mixture.
4. To install the grill grate, position it flat on top of the heating element and gently press down until it sits into place. Place Air Crisp Basket on grill grate, then close the hood.
5. While holding the smoke box lid open, use the pellet scoop to pour pellets into the smoke box until filled to the top. Then close the smoke box lid.
6. Turn dial to AIR CRISP. Press WOODFIRE FLAVOR. Set temperature to 375°F, and set time to 12 minutes. Select START/STOP to begin preheating (preheating will take approx. 8–10 minutes).
7. When unit beeps to signify it has preheated and ADD FOOD is displayed, open hood and place the steaks in basket. Close hood to begin cooking.
8. With 6 minutes remaining, open hood and use silicone-tipped tongs to flip the steaks.
9. When cooking is complete, open hood, remove the steaks from basket, and cut into desired size slices to serve.

Beef Bratwursts

4 (3-ounce / 85-g) beef bratwursts

1. To install the grill grate, position it flat on top of the heating element and gently press down until it sits into place, then close the hood.
2. While holding the smoke box lid open, use the pellet scoop to pour pellets into the smoke box until filled to the top. Then close the smoke box lid.
3. Turn dial to GRILL. Press WOODFIRE FLAVOR. Set temperature to HI, and set time to 6 minutes. Select START/STOP to begin preheating (preheating will take approx. 15–19 minutes).
4. When unit beeps to signify it has preheated and ADD FOOD is displayed, open hood and place the beef bratwursts on grill grate, gently pressing them down to maximize grill marks. Close the hood and grill for 3 minutes. Then open hood, flip the beef bratwursts, and grill for another 3 minutes.
5. When cooking is complete, open hood, remove the beef bratwursts from grill. Serve hot.

PREP: 5 minutes
PREHEAT: approx. 15-19 minutes
TOTAL COOK TIME: 6 minutes

Grilled Skirt Steak

1 cup fresh parsley leaves, chopped finely
3 tbsps. fresh oregano, chopped finely
3 tbsps. fresh mint leaves, chopped finely
2 (8-ounce) skirt steaks
3 garlic cloves, minced
1 tbsp. ground cumin
2 tsps. smoked paprika
1 tsp. cayenne pepper
1 tsp. red pepper flakes, crushed
Salt and freshly ground black pepper, to taste
¾ cup olive oil
3 tbsps. red wine vinegar

PREP: 15 minutes
PREHEAT: approx. 15-19 minutes
TOTAL COOK TIME: 8 minutes

1. Season the steaks with a little salt and black pepper.
2. Mix all the ingredients in a large bowl except the steaks.
3. Put ¼ cup of the herb mixture and steaks in a resealable bag and shake well.
4. Refrigerate for about 24 hours and reserve the remaining herb mixture.
5. Keep the steaks at room temperature for about 30 minutes.
6. To install the grill grate, position it flat on top of the heating element and gently press down until it sits into place, then close the hood.
7. While holding the smoke box lid open, use the pellet scoop to pour pellets into the smoke box until filled to the top. Then close the smoke box lid.
8. Turn dial to GRILL. Press WOODFIRE FLAVOR. Set temperature to MED, and set time to 8 minutes. Select START/STOP to begin preheating (preheating will take approx. 15–19 minutes).
9. When unit beeps to signify it has preheated and ADD FOOD is displayed, open hood and place the steaks on grill grate, gently pressing them down to maximize grill marks. Close the hood and grill for 4 minutes. Then open hood, flip the steaks, and grill for another 4 minutes.
10. When cooking is complete, open hood, remove the steaks from grill. Serve sprinkled with remaining herb mixture to serve.

Grilled Ribeye Steaks

PREP: 10 minutes
PREHEAT: approx. 15-19 minutes
TOTAL COOK TIME: 10 minutes

¼ cup coconut butter
1 clove garlic, minced
Salt and ground black pepper, to taste

1½ tbsps. balsamic vinegar
¼ cup rosemary, chopped
2 ribeye steaks

1. Melt the butter in a skillet over medium heat. Add the garlic and fry until fragrant.
2. Remove the skillet from the heat and add the salt, pepper, and vinegar. Allow it to cool.
3. Add the rosemary, then pour the mixture into a Ziploc bag.
4. Put the ribeye steaks in the bag and shake well, coating the meat well. Refrigerate for an hour, then allow to sit for a further twenty minutes.
5. To install the grill grate, position it flat on top of the heating element and gently press down until it sits into place, then close the hood.
6. While holding the smoke box lid open, use the pellet scoop to pour pellets into the smoke box until filled to the top. Then close the smoke box lid.
7. Turn dial to GRILL. Press WOODFIRE FLAVOR. Set temperature to HI, and set time to 10 minutes. Select START/STOP to begin preheating (preheating will take approx. 15–19 minutes).
8. When unit beeps to signify it has preheated and ADD FOOD is displayed, open hood and place the ribeyes on grill grate, gently pressing them down to maximize grill marks. Close the hood and grill for 5 minutes. Then open hood, flip the ribeyes, and grill for another 5 minutes.
9. When cooking is complete, open hood, remove the ribeyes from grill. Serve hot.

Smoked Beef

PREP: 10 minutes
TOTAL COOK TIME: 4 hours

2½ pounds beef eye of round roast, trimmed
2 tbsps. olive oil
½ tsp. onion powder
½ tsp. garlic powder
½ tsp. cayenne pepper
½ tsp. ground black pepper
Salt, to taste

1. Rub the roast generously with all the spices and coat with olive oil.
2. To install the grill grate, position it flat on top of the heating element and gently press down until it sits into place.
3. Place the roast on the grill grate, then close the hood.
4. While holding the smoke box lid open, use the pellet scoop to pour pellets into the smoke box until filled to the top. Then close the smoke box lid.
5. Turn dial to SMOKER and set temperature to 250°F, and set time to 4 hours. Select START/ STOP to begin cooking (preheating is not needed).
6. Cooking is complete when an instant-read thermometer reads 203°F. When cooking is complete, open hood, remove the roast from grill. Cut into desired size slices to serve.

CHAPTER 6: PORK

Mexican Pork Chops

SERVES: 2

¼ tsp. dried oregano
1½ tsps. taco seasoning mix
2 (4-ounce / 113-g) boneless pork chops
2 tbsps. unsalted butter, divided

PREP: 5 minutes
PREHEAT: approx. 15-19 minutes
TOTAL COOK TIME: 10 minutes

1. Combine the dried oregano and taco seasoning in a small bowl and rub the mixture into the pork chops. Brush the chops with 1 tbsp. butter.
2. To install the grill grate, position it flat on top of the heating element and gently press down until it sits into place, then close the hood.
3. While holding the smoke box lid open, use the pellet scoop to pour pellets into the smoke box until filled to the top. Then close the smoke box lid.
4. Turn dial to GRILL. Press WOODFIRE FLAVOR. Set temperature to HI, and set time to 10 minutes. Select START/STOP to begin preheating (preheating will take approx. 15–19 minutes).
5. When unit beeps to signify it has preheated and ADD FOOD is displayed, open hood and place the chops on grill grate, gently pressing them down to maximize grill marks. Close the hood and grill for 5 minutes. Then open hood, flip the chops, and grill for another 5 minutes.
6. When cooking is complete, open hood, remove the chops from grill. Serve with a garnish of remaining butter.

Orange Pork Tenderloin

SERVES: 3

2 tbsps. coconut sugar
2 tsps. cornstarch
2 tsps. Dijon mustard
½ cup orange juice
½ tsp. soy sauce
2 tsps. grated fresh ginger
¼ cup white wine

Zest of 1 orange
1 pound (454 g) pork tenderloin
Salt and freshly ground black pepper, to taste
Oranges, halved, for garnish
Fresh parsley, for garnish

PREP: 15 minutes
PREHEAT: approx. 15-19 minutes
TOTAL COOK TIME: 18 minutes

1. Combine the coconut sugar, cornstarch, Dijon mustard, orange juice, soy sauce, ginger, white wine and orange zest in a small saucepan and bring the mixture to a boil on the stovetop. Lower the heat and simmer while you cook the pork tenderloin or until the sauce has thickened.
2. Season all sides of the pork tenderloin with salt and freshly ground black pepper.
3. To install the grill grate, position it flat on top of the heating element and gently press down until it sits into place, then close the hood.
4. While holding the smoke box lid open, use the pellet scoop to pour pellets into the smoke box until filled to the top. Then close the smoke box lid.
5. Turn dial to GRILL. Press WOODFIRE FLAVOR. Set temperature to MED, and set time to 18 minutes. Select START/STOP to begin preheating (preheating will take approx. 15–19 minutes).
6. When unit beeps to signify it has preheated and ADD FOOD is displayed, open hood and place the tenderloin on grill grate, gently pressing it down to maximize grill marks. Close the hood and grill for 9 minutes. Then open hood, flip the tenderloin and baste with the sauce. Grill for another 9 minutes.
7. When cooking is complete, open hood, remove the tenderloin from grill. Transfer the tenderloin to a cutting board and let it rest for 5 minutes. Slice the pork at a slight angle and garnish with orange halves and fresh parsley. Serve immediately.

BBQ Pork Steaks

SERVES: 4

PREP: 5 minutes
PREHEAT: approx. 15-19 minutes
TOTAL COOK TIME: 10 minutes

4 pork steaks
1 tbsp. Cajun seasoning
2 tbsps. BBQ sauce
1 tbsp. vinegar
1 tsp. soy sauce
½ cup brown sugar
½ cup ketchup

1. Sprinkle pork steaks with Cajun seasoning.
2. Combine remaining ingredients and brush onto steaks.
3. To install the grill grate, position it flat on top of the heating element and gently press down until it sits into place, then close the hood.
4. While holding the smoke box lid open, use the pellet scoop to pour pellets into the smoke box until filled to the top. Then close the smoke box lid.
5. Turn dial to GRILL. Press WOODFIRE FLAVOR. Set temperature to HI, and set time to 10 minutes. Select START/STOP to begin preheating (preheating will take approx. 15–19 minutes).
6. When unit beeps to signify it has preheated and ADD FOOD is displayed, open hood and place the steaks on grill grate, gently pressing them down to maximize grill marks. Close the hood and grill for 5 minutes. Then open hood, flip the steaks, and grill for another 5 minutes.
7. When cooking is complete, open hood, remove the steaks from grill. Serve hot.

Bacon-Wrapped Jalapeño Poppers

SERVES: 6

PREP: 5 minutes
PREHEAT: approx. 3 minutes
TOTAL COOK TIME: 10 minutes

6 large jalapeños
4 ounces (113 g) ⅓-less-fat cream cheese
¼ cup shredded reduced-fat sharp Cheddar cheese
2 scallions, green tops only, sliced
6 slices center-cut bacon, halved

1. Wearing rubber gloves, halve the jalapeños lengthwise to make 12 pieces. Scoop out the seeds and membranes and discard.
2. In a medium bowl, combine the cream cheese, Cheddar, and scallions. Using a small spoon or spatula, fill the jalapeños with the cream cheese filling. Wrap a bacon strip around each pepper and secure with a toothpick.
3. To install the grill grate, position it flat on top of the heating element and gently press down until it sits into place. Place Air Crisp Basket on grill grate, then close the hood.
4. Turn dial to AIR CRISP. Set temperature to 400°F, and set time to 10 minutes. Select START/STOP to begin preheating (preheating will take approx. 3 minutes).
5. When unit beeps to signify it has preheated and ADD FOOD is displayed, open hood and place stuffed peppers in basket. Close hood to begin cooking.
6. When cooking is complete, open hood, remove stuffed peppers from basket, and serve.

Citrus Smoked Pork Loin

SERVES: 6

1 tbsp. lime juice
1 tbsp. orange marmalade
1 tsp. coarse brown mustard
1 tsp. curry powder
1 tsp. dried lemongrass
2 pound (907 g) boneless pork loin roast
Salt and ground black pepper, to taste
Cooking spray

PREP: 10 minutes
TOTAL COOK TIME: 3 hours

1. Mix the lime juice, marmalade, mustard, curry powder, and lemongrass.
2. Rub mixture all over the surface of the pork loin. Season with salt and pepper.
3. To install the grill grate, position it flat on top of the heating element and gently press down until it sits into place.
4. Place the pork roast on the grill grate, then close the hood.
5. While holding the smoke box lid open, use the pellet scoop to pour pellets into the smoke box until filled to the top. Then close the smoke box lid.
6. Turn dial to SMOKER and set temperature to 250°F, and set time to 3 hours. Select START/ STOP to begin cooking (preheating is not needed).
7. Cooking is complete when an instant-read thermometer reads 180°F. When cooking is complete, open hood, remove the pork roast from grill, and let rest for 20 minutes. Then shred the pork roast and serve.

Grilled Baby Back Ribs

SERVES: 2

2 tsps. red pepper flakes
¾ ground ginger
3 cloves minced garlic
Salt and ground black pepper, to taste
2 baby back ribs

PREP: 5 minutes
PREHEAT: approx. 15-19 minutes
TOTAL COOK TIME: 35 minutes

1. Combine the red pepper flakes, ginger, garlic, salt and pepper in a bowl, making sure to mix well. Massage the mixture into the baby back ribs.
2. To install the grill grate, position it flat on top of the heating element and gently press down until it sits into place, then close the hood.
3. While holding the smoke box lid open, use the pellet scoop to pour pellets into the smoke box until filled to the top. Then close the smoke box lid.
4. Turn dial to GRILL. Press WOODFIRE FLAVOR. Set temperature to HI, and set time to 35 minutes. Select START/STOP to begin preheating (preheating will take approx. 15–19 minutes).
5. When unit beeps to signify it has preheated and ADD FOOD is displayed, open hood and place the ribs on grill grate, gently pressing them down to maximize grill marks. Close the hood and grill for 20 minutes. Then open hood, flip the ribs, and grill for another 15 minutes.
6. When cooking is complete, open hood, remove the ribs from grill. Serve hot.

Pork with Aloha Salsa

SERVES: 4

PREP: 20 minutes
PREHEAT: approx. 8-10 minutes
TOTAL COOK TIME: 12 minutes

2 eggs
2 tbsps. milk
¼ cup flour
¼ cup panko bread crumbs
4 tsps. sesame seeds
1 pound (454 g) boneless, thin
    pork cutlets (⅜- to ½-inch thick)
Lemon pepper and salt, to taste
¼ cup cornstarch
Cooking spray

For the Aloha Salsa:
1 cup fresh pineapple, chopped in
    small pieces
¼ cup red onion, finely chopped
¼ cup green or red bell pepper,
    chopped
½ tsp. ground cinnamon
1 tsp. low-sodium soy sauce
⅛ tsp. crushed red pepper
⅛ tsp. ground black pepper

1. In a medium bowl, stir together all ingredients for salsa. Cover and refrigerate while cooking the pork.
2. Beat the eggs and milk in a shallow dish.
3. In another shallow dish, mix the flour, panko, and sesame seeds.
4. Sprinkle pork cutlets with lemon pepper and salt.
5. Dip pork cutlets in cornstarch, egg mixture, and then panko coating. Spray both sides with cooking spray.
6. To install the grill grate, position it flat on top of the heating element and gently press down until it sits into place. Place Air Crisp Basket on grill grate, then close the hood.
7. While holding the smoke box lid open, use the pellet scoop to pour pellets into the smoke box until filled to the top. Then close the smoke box lid.
8. Turn dial to AIR CRISP. Press WOODFIRE FLAVOR. Set temperature to 390°F, and set time to 12 minutes. Select START/STOP to begin preheating (preheating will take approx. 8–10 minutes).
9. When unit beeps to signify it has preheated and ADD FOOD is displayed, open hood and place the pork cutlets in basket. Close hood to begin cooking.
10. With 6 minutes remaining, open hood and use silicone-tipped tongs to flip the pork cutlets.
11. When cooking is complete, open hood, remove the pork cutlets from basket. Serve with salsa on the side.

Smoked Pork Tenderloin

SERVES: 4-6

PREP: 10 minutes
TOTAL COOK TIME: 35 minutes

¼ cup olive oil
¼ cup soy sauce
¼ cup freshly squeezed lemon
    juice
1 garlic clove, minced

1 tbsp. Dijon mustard
1 tsp. salt
½ tsp. freshly ground black pepper
2 pounds (907 g) pork tenderloin

1. In a large mixing bowl, make the marinade: Mix the olive oil, soy sauce, lemon juice, minced garlic, Dijon mustard, salt, and pepper. Reserve ¼ cup of the marinade.
2. Put the tenderloin in a large bowl and pour the remaining marinade over the meat. Cover and marinate in the refrigerator for about 1 hour.
3. To install the grill grate, position it flat on top of the heating element and gently press down until it sits into place.
4. Place the pork on the grill grate, then close the hood.
5. While holding the smoke box lid open, use the pellet scoop to pour pellets into the smoke box until filled to the top. Then close the smoke box lid.
6. Turn dial to SMOKER and set temperature to 300°F, and set time to 35 minutes. Select START/ STOP to begin cooking (preheating is not needed).
7. After 10 minutes, flip the pork over and baste it with half of the reserved marinade. With 10 minutes, flip the pork over and baste it with the remaining marinade.
8. Cooking is complete when an instant-read thermometer reads 145°F. When cooking is complete, open hood, remove the pork from grill, and let rest for 20 minutes. Serve.

Cheese Crusted Chops

SERVES: 4-6

¼ tsp. pepper
½ tsp. salt
4 to 6 thick boneless pork chops
1 cup pork rind crumbs
¼ tsp. chili powder

½ tsp. onion powder
1 tsp. smoked paprika
2 beaten eggs
3 tbsps. grated Parmesan cheese
Cooking spray

PREP: 10 minutes
PREHEAT: approx. 8-10 minutes
TOTAL COOK TIME: 22 minutes

1. Rub the pepper and salt on both sides of pork chops.
2. In a food processor, pulse pork rinds into crumbs. Mix crumbs with chili powder, onion powder, and paprika in a bowl.
3. Beat eggs in another bowl.
4. Dip pork chops into eggs then into pork rind crumb mixture.
5. To install the grill grate, position it flat on top of the heating element and gently press down until it sits into place. Place Air Crisp Basket on grill grate, then close the hood.
6. While holding the smoke box lid open, use the pellet scoop to pour pellets into the smoke box until filled to the top. Then close the smoke box lid.
7. Turn dial to AIR CRISP. Press WOODFIRE FLAVOR. Set temperature to 390°F, and set time to 22 minutes. Select START/STOP to begin preheating (preheating will take approx. 8–10 minutes).
8. When unit beeps to signify it has preheated and ADD FOOD is displayed, open hood. Spritz the basket with cooking spray and add pork chops to basket. Close hood to begin cooking.
9. With 11 minutes remaining, open hood and use silicone-tipped tongs to flip the pork chops.
10. When cooking is complete, open hood, remove the pork chops from basket, and serve garnished with the Parmesan cheese.

Sun-dried Tomato Crusted Chops

SERVES: 4

½ cup oil-packed sun-dried tomatoes
½ cup toasted almonds
¼ cup grated Parmesan cheese
½ cup olive oil, plus more for brushing

2 tbsps. water
½ tsp. salt
Freshly ground black pepper, to taste
4 center-cut boneless pork chops (about 1¼ pounds / 567 g)

PREP: 15 minutes
PREHEAT: approx. 15-19 minutes
TOTAL COOK TIME: 12 minutes

1. Put the sun-dried tomatoes into a food processor and pulse them until they are coarsely chopped. Add the almonds, Parmesan cheese, olive oil, water, salt and pepper. Process into a smooth paste.
2. Spread most of the paste (leave a little in reserve) onto both sides of the pork chops and then pierce the meat several times with a needle-style meat tenderizer or a fork. Let the pork chops sit and marinate for at least 1 hour (refrigerate if marinating for longer than 1 hour).
3. To install the grill grate, position it flat on top of the heating element and gently press down until it sits into place, then close the hood.
4. While holding the smoke box lid open, use the pellet scoop to pour pellets into the smoke box until filled to the top. Then close the smoke box lid.
5. Turn dial to GRILL. Press WOODFIRE FLAVOR. Set temperature to HI, and set time to 12 minutes. Select START/STOP to begin preheating (preheating will take approx. 15–19 minutes).
6. When unit beeps to signify it has preheated and ADD FOOD is displayed, open hood. Brush more olive oil on the grill and place the pork chops on grill grate, gently pressing them down to maximize grill marks. Close the hood and grill for 6 minutes. Then open hood, flip the pork chops, and grill for another 6 minutes.
7. When cooking is complete, open hood, remove the pork chops from grill. Serve hot.

Glazed Smoked Pork Tenderloin

SERVES: 5

PREP: 5 minutes
TOTAL COOK TIME: 35 minutes

2 pounds pork tenderloin
½ cup Carolina Gold Sauce

1. Liberally coat pork on all sides with Carolina Gold Sauce.
2. To install the grill grate, position it flat on top of the heating element and gently press down until it sits into place.
3. Place the pork on the grill grate, then close the hood.
4. While holding the smoke box lid open, use the pellet scoop to pour pellets into the smoke box until filled to the top. Then close the smoke box lid.
5. Turn dial to SMOKER and set temperature to 300°F, and set time to 35 minutes. Select START/ STOP to begin cooking (preheating is not needed).
6. Cooking is complete when an instant-read thermometer reads 145°F. When cooking is complete, open hood, remove the pork from grill, and let rest for 30 minutes. Then shred the pork and serve with the remaining sauce.

   Carolina Gold Sauce: 1 cup yellow mustard, ¼ cup apple cider vinegar, ¼ cup honey, 1 tbsp. Worcestershire sauce, 1 tbsp. soy sauce, 1 tbsp. chili powder, 1 tsp. garlic powder, kosher salt as desired, ground black pepper as desired

Bourbon Barbecue–Glazed Pork Chops

SERVES: 4

PREP: 5 minutes
PREHEAT: approx. 15-19 minutes
TOTAL COOK TIME: 32 minutes

2 cups ketchup
¾ cup bourbon
¼ cup apple cider vinegar
¼ cup soy sauce
1 cup packed brown sugar

3 tbsps. Worcestershire sauce
½ tbsp. dry mustard powder
4 boneless pork chops
Sea salt
Freshly ground black pepper

1. In a medium saucepan over high heat, combine the ketchup, bourbon, vinegar, soy sauce, sugar, Worcestershire sauce, and mustard powder. Stir to combine and bring to a boil.
2. Reduce the heat to low and simmer, uncovered and stirring occasionally, for 20 minutes. The barbecue sauce will thicken while cooking. Once thickened, remove the pan from the heat and set aside.
3. To install the grill grate, position it flat on top of the heating element and gently press down until it sits into place, then close the hood.
4. While holding the smoke box lid open, use the pellet scoop to pour pellets into the smoke box until filled to the top. Then close the smoke box lid.
5. Turn dial to GRILL. Press WOODFIRE FLAVOR. Set temperature to HI, and set time to 12 minutes. Select START/STOP to begin preheating (preheating will take approx. 15–19 minutes).
6. When unit beeps to signify it has preheated and ADD FOOD is displayed, open hood and place the pork chops on grill grate, gently pressing them down to maximize grill marks. Close the hood and grill for 4 minutes. Then open hood, flip the pork chops and baste the cooked side with the barbecue sauce. Grill for another 6 minutes, flip the pork chops again, basting both sides with the barbecue sauce. Close the hood to continue cooking for 2 minutes.
7. When cooking is complete, open hood, remove the pork chops from grill. Season with salt and pepper and serve immediately.

Cheesy Sausage Balls

SERVES: 6

12 ounces (340 g) Jimmy Dean's Sausage
6 ounces (170 g) shredded Cheddar cheese
12 Cheddar cubes

1. Mix the shredded cheese and sausage.
2. Divide the mixture into 12 equal parts to be stuffed.
3. Add a cube of cheese to the center of the sausage and roll into balls.
4. To install the grill grate, position it flat on top of the heating element and gently press down until it sits into place. Place Air Crisp Basket on grill grate, then close the hood.
5. While holding the smoke box lid open, use the pellet scoop to pour pellets into the smoke box until filled to the top. Then close the smoke box lid.
6. Turn dial to AIR CRISP. Press WOODFIRE FLAVOR. Set temperature to 375°F, and set time to 15 minutes. Select START/STOP to begin preheating (preheating will take approx. 8–10 minutes).
7. When unit beeps to signify it has preheated and ADD FOOD is displayed, open hood and place the balls in basket. Close hood to begin cooking, shaking frequently during cooking.
8. When cooking is complete, open hood, remove the balls from basket, and serve.

PREP: 5 minutes
PREHEAT: approx. 8-10 minutes
TOTAL COOK TIME: 15 minutes

Baked Chorizo Scotch Eggs

SERVES: 4

1 pound (454 g) Mexican chorizo
or other seasoned sausage
meat
4 soft-boiled eggs plus 1 raw egg

1 tbsp. water
½ cup all-purpose flour
1 cup panko bread crumbs
Cooking spray

1. Divide the chorizo into 4 equal portions. Flatten each portion into a disc. Place a soft-boiled egg in the center of each disc. Wrap the chorizo around the egg, encasing it completely. Place the encased eggs on a plate and chill for at least 30 minutes.
2. Beat the raw egg with 1 tbsp. of water. Place the flour on a small plate and the panko on a second plate. Working with 1 egg at a time, roll the encased egg in the flour, then dip it in the egg mixture. Dredge the egg in the panko and place on a plate. Repeat with the remaining eggs.
3. To install the grill grate, position it flat on top of the heating element and gently press down until it sits into place. Place Air Crisp Basket on grill grate, then close the hood.
4. While holding the smoke box lid open, use the pellet scoop to pour pellets into the smoke box until filled to the top. Then close the smoke box lid.
5. Turn dial to BAKE. Press WOODFIRE FLAVOR. Set temperature to 360°F, and set time to 16 minutes. Select START/STOP to begin preheating (preheating will take approx. 8–10 minutes).
6. When unit beeps to signify it has preheated and ADD FOOD is displayed, open hood and place the eggs in basket. Close hood to begin cooking.
7. With 8 minutes remaining, open hood and use silicone-tipped tongs to flip the eggs.
8. When cooking is complete, open hood, remove the eggs from basket, and serve.

PREP: 5 minutes
PREHEAT: approx. 8-10 minutes
TOTAL COOK TIME: 16 minutes

Barbecue Pork Ribs

PREP: 5 minutes
PREHEAT: approx. 15-19 minutes
TOTAL COOK TIME: 30 minutes

1 tbsp. barbecue dry rub
1 tsp. mustard
1 tbsp. apple cider vinegar
1 tsp. sesame oil
1 pound (454 g) pork ribs, chopped

1. Combine the dry rub, mustard, apple cider vinegar, and sesame oil, then coat the ribs with this mixture. Refrigerate the ribs for 20 minutes.
2. To install the grill grate, position it flat on top of the heating element and gently press down until it sits into place, then close the hood.
3. While holding the smoke box lid open, use the pellet scoop to pour pellets into the smoke box until filled to the top. Then close the smoke box lid.
4. Turn dial to GRILL. Press WOODFIRE FLAVOR. Set temperature to HI, and set time to 30 minutes. Select START/STOP to begin preheating (preheating will take approx. 15–19 minutes).
5. When unit beeps to signify it has preheated and ADD FOOD is displayed, open hood and place the ribs on grill grate, gently pressing them down to maximize grill marks. Close the hood and grill for 15 minutes. Then open hood, flip the ribs, and grill for another 15 minutes.
6. When cooking is complete, open hood, remove the ribs from grill. Serve hot.

Simple Pulled Pork

PREP: 5 minutes
PREHEAT: approx. 15-19 minutes
TOTAL COOK TIME: 18 minutes

2 tbsps. barbecue dry rub
1 pound (454 g) pork tenderloin
⅓ cup heavy cream
1 tsp. butter

1. Massage the dry rub into the tenderloin, coating it well.
2. To install the grill grate, position it flat on top of the heating element and gently press down until it sits into place, then close the hood.
3. While holding the smoke box lid open, use the pellet scoop to pour pellets into the smoke box until filled to the top. Then close the smoke box lid.
4. Turn dial to GRILL. Press WOODFIRE FLAVOR. Set temperature to MED, and set time to 18 minutes. Select START/STOP to begin preheating (preheating will take approx. 15–19 minutes).
5. When unit beeps to signify it has preheated and ADD FOOD is displayed, open hood and place the tenderloin on grill grate, gently pressing it down to maximize grill marks. Close the hood and grill for 14 minutes. Then open hood, shred the tenderloin with two forks. Add the heavy cream and butter into the basket along with the shredded pork and stir well. Grill for another 4 minutes.
6. When cooking is complete, open hood, remove the pork from grill. Allow to cool and serve.

CHAPTER 7: LAMB

Grilled Lamb Chops

SERVES: 2

4 (4-ounces) lamb chops
1 tbsp. fresh lemon juice
1 tbsp. olive oil
1 tsp. dried rosemary
1 tsp. dried thyme

1 tsp. dried oregano
½ tsp. ground cumin
½ tsp. ground coriander
Salt and black pepper, to taste

PREP: 10 minutes
PREHEAT: approx. 15-19 minutes
TOTAL COOK TIME: 8 minutes

1. Mix the lemon juice, oil, herbs, and spices in a large bowl.
2. Coat the chops generously with the herb mixture and refrigerate to marinate for about 1 hour.
3. To install the grill grate, position it flat on top of the heating element and gently press down until it sits into place, then close the hood.
4. While holding the smoke box lid open, use the pellet scoop to pour pellets into the smoke box until filled to the top. Then close the smoke box lid.
5. Turn dial to GRILL. Press WOODFIRE FLAVOR. Set temperature to HI, and set time to 8 minutes. Select START/STOP to begin preheating (preheating will take approx. 15–19 minutes).
6. When unit beeps to signify it is preheated and ADD FOOD is displayed, open hood and add the chops to the grill plate. Close the hood and grill for 4 minutes. Then open hood, flip chops, and grill for another 4 minutes.
7. When cooking is complete, open hood, remove chops from grill. Serve hot.

Fast Lamb Satay

SERVES: 2

¼ tsp. cumin
1 tsp. ginger
½ tsp. nutmeg
Salt and ground black pepper, to taste
2 boneless lamb steaks
Cooking spray

PREP: 5 minutes
PREHEAT: approx. 15-19 minutes
TOTAL COOK TIME: 8 minutes

1. Combine the cumin, ginger, nutmeg, salt and pepper in a bowl.
2. Cube the lamb steaks and massage the spice mixture into each one.
3. Leave to marinate for 10 minutes, then transfer onto metal skewers.
4. To install the grill grate, position it flat on top of the heating element and gently press down until it sits into place, then close the hood.
5. While holding the smoke box lid open, use the pellet scoop to pour pellets into the smoke box until filled to the top. Then close the smoke box lid.
6. Turn dial to GRILL. Press WOODFIRE FLAVOR. Set temperature to HI, and set time to 10 minutes. Select START/STOP to begin preheating (preheating will take approx. 15–19 minutes).
7. When unit beeps to signify it has preheated and ADD FOOD is displayed, open hood and place the skewers on grill grate, gently pressing them down to maximize grill marks. Close the hood and grill for 4 minutes. Then open hood, flip the skewers, and grill for another 4 minutes.
8. When cooking is complete, open hood, remove the skewers from grill. Serve hot.

Grilled Rack of Lamb Chops

PREP: 5 minutes
PREHEAT: approx. 15-19 minutes
TOTAL COOK TIME: 14 minutes

3 tbsps. extra-virgin olive oil
1 garlic clove, minced
1 tbsp. fresh rosemary, chopped
½ rack lamb (4 bones)
Sea salt
Freshly ground black pepper

1. Combine the oil, garlic, and rosemary in a large bowl. Season the rack of lamb with the salt and pepper, then place the lamb in the bowl, using tongs to turn and coat fully in the oil mixture. Cover and refrigerate for 2 hours.
2. To install the grill grate, position it flat on top of the heating element and gently press down until it sits into place, then close the hood.
3. While holding the smoke box lid open, use the pellet scoop to pour pellets into the smoke box until filled to the top. Then close the smoke box lid.
4. Turn dial to GRILL. Press WOODFIRE FLAVOR. Set temperature to HI, and set time to 10 minutes. Select START/STOP to begin preheating (preheating will take approx. 15–19 minutes).
5. When unit beeps to signify it has preheated and ADD FOOD is displayed, open hood and place the lamb on grill grate, gently pressing it down to maximize grill marks. Close the hood and grill for 7 minutes. Then open hood, flip the lamb, and grill for another 7 minutes.
6. When cooking is complete, open hood, remove the lamb from grill. Serve hot.

Lollipop Lamb Rack

PREP: 15 minutes
PREHEAT: approx. 15-19 minutes
TOTAL COOK TIME: 16 minutes

1 lamb rack
½ small clove garlic
¼ cup packed fresh parsley
¾ cup packed fresh mint
½ tsp. lemon juice
¼ cup grated Parmesan cheese
⅓ cup shelled pistachios
¼ tsp. salt
½ cup olive oil
2 tbsps. vegetable oil
Salt and freshly ground black pepper, to taste
1 tbsp. dried rosemary, chopped
1 tbsp. dried thyme

1. Make the pesto by combining the garlic, parsley and mint in a food processor and process until finely chopped. Add the lemon juice, Parmesan cheese, pistachios and salt. Process until all the ingredients have turned into a paste. With the processor running, slowly pour the olive oil in. Scrape the sides of the processor with a spatula and process for another 30 seconds.
2. Rub both sides of the lamb rack with vegetable oil and season with salt, pepper, rosemary and thyme, pressing the herbs into the meat gently with the fingers.
3. To install the grill grate, position it flat on top of the heating element and gently press down until it sits into place, then close the hood.
4. While holding the smoke box lid open, use the pellet scoop to pour pellets into the smoke box until filled to the top. Then close the smoke box lid.
5. Turn dial to GRILL. Press WOODFIRE FLAVOR. Set temperature to HI, and set time to 16 minutes. Select START/STOP to begin preheating (preheating will take approx. 15–19 minutes).
6. When unit beeps to signify it has preheated and ADD FOOD is displayed, open hood and place the lamb rack on grill grate, gently pressing it down to maximize grill marks. Close the hood and grill for 8 minutes. Then open hood, flip lamb rack, and grill for another 8 minutes.
7. When cooking is complete, open hood, remove the lamb rack from grill. Serve with mint pesto drizzled on top.

Nut Crusted Rack of Lamb

SERVES: 4

1¾ pounds rack of lamb
1 egg
1 tbsp. breadcrumbs
3-ounce almonds, chopped finely

1 tbsp. fresh rosemary, chopped
1 tbsp. olive oil
1 garlic clove, minced
Salt and black pepper, to taste

PREP: 15 minutes
PREHEAT: approx. 8-10 minutes
TOTAL COOK TIME: 20 minutes

1. Mix garlic, olive oil, salt and black pepper in a bowl.
2. Whisk the egg in a shallow dish and mix breadcrumbs, almonds and rosemary in another shallow dish.
3. Coat the rack of lamb with garlic mixture evenly, dip into the egg and dredge into the breadcrumb mixture.
4. To install the grill grate, position it flat on top of the heating element and gently press down until it sits into place. Place Air Crisp Basket on grill grate, then close the hood.
5. While holding the smoke box lid open, use the pellet scoop to pour pellets into the smoke box until filled to the top. Then close the smoke box lid.
6. Turn dial to ROAST. Press WOODFIRE FLAVOR. Set temperature to 390°F, and set time to 20 minutes. Select START/STOP to begin preheating (preheating will take approx. 8–10 minutes).
7. When unit beeps to signify it has preheated and ADD FOOD is displayed, open hood and place the rack of lamb in basket. Close hood to begin cooking.
8. With 10 minutes remaining, open hood and use silicone-tipped tongs to flip the rack of lamb.
9. When cooking is complete, open hood, remove the rack of lamb from basket, and serve.

Crispy Lamb Ribs

SERVES: 2

2 tbsps. mustard
1 pound (454 g) lamb ribs
1 tsp. rosemary, chopped

Salt and ground black pepper, to taste
¼ cup mint leaves, chopped
1 cup Greek yogurt

PREP: 5 minutes
PREHEAT: approx. 8-10 minutes
TOTAL COOK TIME: 16 minutes

1. Use a brush to apply the mustard to the lamb ribs, and season with rosemary, salt, and pepper.
2. To install the grill grate, position it flat on top of the heating element and gently press down until it sits into place. Place Air Crisp Basket on grill grate, then close the hood.
3. While holding the smoke box lid open, use the pellet scoop to pour pellets into the smoke box until filled to the top. Then close the smoke box lid.
4. Turn dial to AIR CRISP. Press WOODFIRE FLAVOR. Set temperature to 390°F, and set time to 16 minutes. Select START/STOP to begin preheating (preheating will take approx. 8–10 minutes).
5. When unit beeps to signify it has preheated and ADD FOOD is displayed, open hood and place the ribs in basket. Close hood to begin cooking.
6. Meanwhile, combine the mint leaves and yogurt in a bowl.
7. With 8 minutes remaining, open hood and use silicone-tipped tongs to flip the ribs.
8. When cooking is complete, open hood, remove the ribs from basket, and serve with the mint yogurt.

Grilled Lamb Steaks

SERVES: 3

PREP: 15 minutes
PREHEAT: approx. 15-19 minutes
TOTAL COOK TIME: 10 minutes

½ onion, roughly chopped
1½ pounds boneless lamb sirloin
  steaks
5 garlic cloves, peeled
1 tbsp. fresh ginger, peeled
1 tsp. garam masala
1 tsp. ground fennel
½ tsp. ground cumin
½ tsp. ground cinnamon
½ tsp. cayenne pepper
Salt and black pepper, to taste

1. Put the onion, garlic, ginger, and spices in a blender and pulse until smooth.
2. Coat the lamb steaks with this mixture on both sides and refrigerate to marinate for about 24 hours.
3. To install the grill grate, position it flat on top of the heating element and gently press down until it sits into place, then close the hood.
4. While holding the smoke box lid open, use the pellet scoop to pour pellets into the smoke box until filled to the top. Then close the smoke box lid.
5. Turn dial to GRILL. Press WOODFIRE FLAVOR. Set temperature to HI, and set time to 10 minutes. Select START/STOP to begin preheating (preheating will take approx. 15–19 minutes).
6. When unit beeps to signify it has preheated and ADD FOOD is displayed, open hood and place lamb steaks on grill grate, gently pressing them down to maximize grill marks. Close the hood and grill for 5 minutes. Then open hood, flip lamb steaks, and grill for another 5 minutes.
7. When cooking is complete, open hood, remove lamb steaks from grill. Serve hot.

Greek Lamb Pita Pockets

SERVES: 4

PREP: 15 minutes
PREHEAT: approx. 8-10 minutes
TOTAL COOK TIME: 6 minutes

For the Dressing:
1 cup plain yogurt
1 tbsp. lemon juice
1 tsp. dried dill weed, crushed
1 tsp. ground oregano
½ tsp. salt
For the Meatballs:
½ pound (227 g) ground lamb
1 tbsp. diced onion
1 tsp. dried parsley
1 tsp. dried dill weed, crushed
¼ tsp. oregano
¼ tsp. coriander
¼ tsp. ground cumin
¼ tsp. salt
4 pita halves
Suggested Toppings:
1 red onion, slivered
1 medium cucumber, deseeded,
  thinly sliced
Crumbled Feta cheese
Sliced black olives
Chopped fresh peppers

1. Stir the dressing ingredients together in a small bowl and refrigerate while preparing lamb.
2. Combine all meatball ingredients in a large bowl and stir to distribute seasonings.
3. Shape meat mixture into 12 small meatballs, rounded or slightly flattened if you prefer.
4. To install the grill grate, position it flat on top of the heating element and gently press down until it sits into place. Place Air Crisp Basket on grill grate, then close the hood.
5. While holding the smoke box lid open, use the pellet scoop to pour pellets into the smoke box until filled to the top. Then close the smoke box lid.
6. Turn dial to AIR CRISP. Press WOODFIRE FLAVOR. Set temperature to 390°F, and set time to 6 minutes. Select START/STOP to begin preheating (preheating will take approx. 8–10 minutes).
7. When unit beeps to signify it has preheated and ADD FOOD is displayed, open hood and place the meatballs in basket. Close hood to begin cooking.
8. With 3 minutes remaining, open hood and use silicone-tipped tongs to flip the meatballs.
9. When cooking is complete, open hood, remove meatballs from basket, and drain on paper towels.
10. To serve, pile meatballs and the choice of toppings in pita pockets and drizzle with dressing.

Italian Lamb Chops with Avocado Mayo

SERVES: 2

2 lamp chops
2 tsps. Italian herbs
2 avocados

½ cup mayonnaise
1 tbsp. lemon juice

PREP: 5 minutes
PREHEAT: approx. 15-19 minutes
TOTAL COOK TIME: 10 minutes

1. Season the lamb chops with the Italian herbs, then set aside for 5 minutes.
2. To install the grill grate, position it flat on top of the heating element and gently press down until it sits into place, then close the hood.
3. While holding the smoke box lid open, use the pellet scoop to pour pellets into the smoke box until filled to the top. Then close the smoke box lid.
4. Turn dial to GRILL. Press WOODFIRE FLAVOR. Set temperature to MED, and set time to 10 minutes. Select START/STOP to begin preheating (preheating will take approx. 15–19 minutes).
5. When unit beeps to signify it has preheated and ADD FOOD is displayed, open hood and place chops on grill grate, gently pressing them down to maximize grill marks. Close the hood and grill for 5 minutes. Then open hood, flip the chops, and grill for another 5 minutes.
6. In the meantime, halve the avocados and open to remove the pits. Spoon the flesh into a blender. Add the mayonnaise and lemon juice and pulse until a smooth consistency is achieved.
7. When cooking is complete, open hood, remove the chops from grill. Serve with the avocado mayo.

Scrumptious Lamb Chops

SERVES: 4

2 tbsps. fresh mint leaves, minced
4 (6-ounce) lamb chops
2 carrots, peeled and cubed
1 parsnip, peeled and cubed

1 fennel bulb, cubed
1 garlic clove, minced
2 tbsps. dried rosemary
3 tbsps. olive oil
Salt and black pepper, to taste

PREP: 20 minutes
PREHEAT: approx. 15-19 minutes
TOTAL COOK TIME: 25 minutes

1. Mix herbs, garlic and oil in a large bowl and coat lamp chops generously with this mixture.
2. Marinate in the refrigerator for about 3 hours.
3. Soak the vegetables in a large pan of water for about 15 minutes.
4. To install the grill grate, position it flat on top of the heating element and gently press down until it sits into place, then close the hood.
5. While holding the smoke box lid open, use the pellet scoop to pour pellets into the smoke box until filled to the top. Then close the smoke box lid.
6. Turn dial to GRILL. Press WOODFIRE FLAVOR. Set temperature to HI, and set time to 10 minutes. Select START/STOP to begin preheating (preheating will take approx. 15–19 minutes).
7. When unit beeps to signify it has preheated and ADD FOOD is displayed, open hood and place the lamb chops and vegetables on grill grate, gently pressing them down to maximize grill marks. Close the hood and grill for 5 minutes. Then open hood, set the vegetables aside and let cool. Flip the lamb chops and grill for another 5 minutes.
8. When cooking is complete, open hood, remove the lamb from grill. Serve warm.

BBQ Smoked Leg of Lamb

SERVES: 6

PREP: 10 minutes
TOTAL COOK TIME: 6 hours

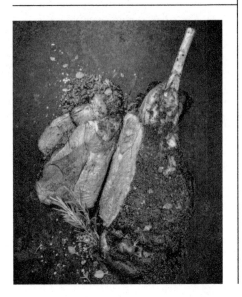

3 pounds leg of lamb
½ cup Basic BBQ Spice Rub
Kosher salt, as desired
Ground black pepper, as desired

1. Liberally season leg of lamb on all sides with Basic BBQ Spice Rub, salt, and pepper.
2. To install the grill grate, position it flat on top of the heating element and gently press down until it sits into place.
3. Place the leg of lamb on the grill grate, then close the hood.
4. While holding the smoke box lid open, use the pellet scoop to pour pellets into the smoke box until filled to the top. Then close the smoke box lid.
5. Turn dial to SMOKER and set temperature to 250°F, and set time to 6 hours. Select START/ STOP to begin cooking (preheating is not needed).
6. Cooking is complete when an instant-read thermometer reads 203°F. When cooking is complete, open hood, remove the leg of lamb from grill, and let rest for 30 minutes. Serve warm.

   Basic BBQ Spice Rub: ¼ cup brown sugar, ¼ cup smoked paprika, 3 tbsps. black pepper, 2 tbsps. kosher salt, 2 tsps. garlic powder, 2 tsps. onion powder

Pesto Coated Rack of Lamb

SERVES: 4

PREP: 15 minutes
PREHEAT: approx. 8-10 minutes
TOTAL COOK TIME: 16 minutes

½ bunch fresh mint
1 (1½-pounds) rack of lamb
1 garlic clove
¼ cup extra-virgin olive oil
½ tbsp. honey
Salt and black pepper, to taste

1. Put the mint, garlic, oil, honey, salt, and black pepper in a blender and pulse until smooth to make pesto.
2. Coat the rack of lamb with this pesto on both sides.
3. To install the grill grate, position it flat on top of the heating element and gently press down until it sits into place. Place Air Crisp Basket on grill grate, then close the hood.
4. While holding the smoke box lid open, use the pellet scoop to pour pellets into the smoke box until filled to the top. Then close the smoke box lid.
5. Turn dial to ROAST. Press WOODFIRE FLAVOR. Set temperature to 390°F, and set time to 16 minutes. Select START/STOP to begin preheating (preheating will take approx. 8–10 minutes).
6. When unit beeps to signify it has preheated and ADD FOOD is displayed, open hood and place the rack of lamb in basket. Close hood to begin cooking.
7. With 8 minutes remaining, open hood and use silicone-tipped tongs to flip the rack of lamb.
8. When cooking is complete, open hood, remove the rack of lamb from basket. Cut the rack into individual chops to serve.

Simple Grilled Lamb Chops

SERVES: 2

4 (4-ounces) lamb chops
Salt and black pepper, to taste
1 tbsp. olive oil

PREP: 10 minutes
PREHEAT: approx. 15-19 minutes
TOTAL COOK TIME: 10 minutes

1. Mix the olive oil, salt, and black pepper in a large bowl and add chops.
2. To install the grill grate, position it flat on top of the heating element and gently press down until it sits into place, then close the hood.
3. While holding the smoke box lid open, use the pellet scoop to pour pellets into the smoke box until filled to the top. Then close the smoke box lid.
4. Turn dial to GRILL. Press WOODFIRE FLAVOR. Set temperature to MED, and set time to 10 minutes. Select START/STOP to begin preheating (preheating will take approx. 15–19 minutes).
5. When unit beeps to signify it has preheated and ADD FOOD is displayed, open hood and place the lamb chops on grill grate, gently pressing them down to maximize grill marks. Close the hood and grill for 5 minutes. Then open hood, flip the lamb chops, and grill for another 5 minutes.
6. When cooking is complete, open hood, remove the lamb chops from grill. Serve hot.

Smoked Leg of Lamb with Brussels Sprouts

SERVES: 6-8

3 pounds leg of lamb
½ cup Cajun Spice Blend
1 tbsp. fresh rosemary, minced
1 tbsp. fresh lemon thyme
1½ pounds Brussels sprouts, trimmed

3 tbsps. olive oil, divided
1 garlic clove, minced
Salt and ground black pepper, as required
2 tbsps. honey

PREP: 20 minutes
TOTAL COOK TIME: 6 hours

1. Make slits in the leg of lamb with a sharp knife. Liberally season leg of lamb on all sides with Cajun Spice Blend.
2. Mix 2 tbsps. of oil, herbs, garlic, salt, and black pepper in a bowl. Coat the Brussels sprouts with oil mixture generously.
3. To install the grill grate, position it flat on top of the heating element and gently press down until it sits into place.
4. Place the leg of lamb and Brussels sprouts on the grill grate, then close the hood.
5. While holding the smoke box lid open, use the pellet scoop to pour pellets into the smoke box until filled to the top. Then close the smoke box lid.
6. Turn dial to SMOKER and set temperature to 250°F, and set time to 6 hours. Select START/ STOP to begin cooking (preheating is not needed). Set an external timer to 25 minutes.
7. After 25 minutes, open hood, remove Brussels sprouts and set aside. Close hood to continue cooking the leg of lamb. Let the Brussels sprouts cool.
8. Cooking is complete when an instant-read thermometer reads 203°F. When cooking is complete, open hood, remove the leg of lamb from grill, and let rest for 30 minutes. Then shred the leg of lamb and serve.

Cajun Spice Blend: 1 tsp. garlic powder, 1 tsp. onion powder, ½ tsp. white pepper, ¼ tsp. cayenne pepper, 1 tsp. kosher salt, 1 tsp. paprika, ½ tsp. thyme, 1 tsp. oregano

Grilled Lamb Meatballs

PREP: 20 minutes
PREHEAT: approx. 15-19 minutes
TOTAL COOK TIME: 10 minutes

For the Meatballs:
1 pound (454 g) ground lamb
½ small onion, finely diced
1 clove garlic, minced
2 tbsps. fresh parsley, finely chopped (plus more for garnish)
2 tsps. fresh oregano, finely chopped
2 tbsps. skim milk
1 egg yolk
Salt and freshly ground black pepper, to taste
½ cup crumbled feta cheese, for garnish
For the Tomato Sauce:
Olive oil, for greasing
1 (28-ounce / 794-g) can crushed tomatoes
2 tbsps. butter
1 clove garlic, smashed
Pinch crushed red pepper flakes
¼ tsp. ground cinnamon
Salt, to taste

1. Combine all ingredients for the meatballs in a large bowl and mix just until everything is combined. Shape the mixture into 1½-inch balls or shape the meat between two spoons to make quenelles.
2. To install the grill grate, position it flat on top of the heating element and gently press down until it sits into place, then close the hood.
3. While holding the smoke box lid open, use the pellet scoop to pour pellets into the smoke box until filled to the top. Then close the smoke box lid.
4. Turn dial to GRILL. Press WOODFIRE FLAVOR. Set temperature to HI, and set time to 10 minutes. Select START/STOP to begin pre-heating (preheating will take approx. 15–19 minutes).
5. Prepare the quick tomato sauce: Put the butter, garlic and red pepper flakes in a sauté pan and heat over medium heat on the stovetop. Let the garlic sizzle a little, but before the butter browns, add the cinnamon and tomatoes. Bring to a simmer and simmer for 15 minutes. Season with salt.
6. When unit beeps to signify it has preheated and ADD FOOD is displayed, open hood and place the meatballs on grill grate, gently pressing them down to maximize grill marks. Spray the meatballs with olive oil, and close hood to begin cooking.
7. Close the hood and grill for 5 minutes. Then open hood, flip the meatballs, and grill for another 5 minutes.
8. When cooking is complete, open hood, remove the meatballs from grill.
9. To serve, spoon a pool of the tomato sauce onto plates and add the meatballs. Sprinkle the feta cheese on top and garnish with more fresh parsley. Serve immediately.

CHAPTER 8: POULTRY

Fajita-Style Chicken Kebabs

SERVES: 4

1 tbsp. ground cumin
1 tbsp. garlic powder
1 tbsp. chili powder
2 tsps. paprika
¼ tsp. sea salt
¼ tsp. freshly ground black pepper
1 pound boneless, skinless chicken

breasts, cut in 2-inch cubes
2 tbsps. extra-virgin olive oil, divided
2 red bell peppers, seeded and cut into 1-inch cubes
1 red onion, quartered
Juice of 1 lime

PREP: 15 minutes
PREHEAT: approx. 15-19 minutes
TOTAL COOK TIME: 12 minutes

1. In a small mixing bowl, combine the cumin, garlic powder, chili powder, paprika, salt, and pepper, and mix well.
2. Place the chicken, 1 tbsp. oil, and half of the spice mixture into a large resealable plastic bag or container. Toss to coat evenly.
3. Place the bell pepper, onion, remaining 1 tbsp. of oil, and remaining spice mixture into a large resealable plastic bag or container. Toss to coat evenly. Refrigerate the chicken and vegetables for at least 30 minutes.
4. To install the grill grate, position it flat on top of the heating element and gently press down until it sits into place, then close the hood.
5. While holding the smoke box lid open, use the pellet scoop to pour pellets into the smoke box until filled to the top. Then close the smoke box lid.
6. Turn dial to GRILL. Press WOODFIRE FLAVOR. Set temperature to HI, and set time to 12 minutes. Select START/STOP to begin preheating (preheating will take approx. 15–19 minutes).
7. Assemble the kebabs by threading the chicken onto the skewers, alternating with the peppers and onion. Ensure the ingredients are pushed almost completely down to the end of the skewers.
8. When unit beeps to signify it has preheated and ADD FOOD is displayed, open hood and place the skewers on grill grate, gently pressing them down to maximize grill marks. Close the hood and grill for 6 minutes. Then open hood, flip the skewers, and grill for another 6 minutes.
9. When cooking is complete, open hood, remove the skewers from grill. Drizzle with lime juice and serve hot.

Piri-Piri Chicken Thighs

SERVES: 4

¼ cup piri-piri sauce
1 tbsp. freshly squeezed lemon juice
2 tbsps. brown sugar, divided
2 cloves garlic, minced

1 tbsp. extra-virgin olive oil
4 bone-in, skin-on chicken thighs, each weighing approximately 7 to 8 ounces (198 to 227 g)
½ tsp. cornstarch

PREP: 5 minutes
TOTAL COOK TIME: 20 minutes

1. To make the marinade, whisk together the piri-piri sauce, lemon juice, 1 tbsp. of brown sugar, and the garlic in a small bowl. While whisking, slowly pour in the oil in a steady stream and continue to whisk until emulsified. Using a skewer, poke holes in the chicken thighs and place them in a small glass dish. Pour the marinade over the chicken and turn the thighs to coat them with the sauce. Cover the dish and refrigerate for at least 15 minutes and up to 1 hour.
2. To install the grill grate, position it flat on top of the heating element and gently press down until it sits into place.
3. Remove the chicken thighs from the dish, reserving the marinade, and place them skin-side down on the grill grate, then close the hood.
4. While holding the smoke box lid open, use the pellet scoop to pour pellets into the smoke box until filled to the top. Then close the smoke box lid.
5. Turn dial to SMOKER and set temperature to 375°F, and set time to 20 minutes. Select START/ STOP to begin cooking (preheating is not needed).
6. Meanwhile, whisk the remaining brown sugar and the cornstarch into the marinade and microwave it on high power for 1 minute until it is bubbling and thickened to a glaze.
7. With 10 minutes remaining, open the hood and brush the chicken thighs with the glaze.
8. Cooking is complete when an instant-read thermometer reads 165°F. When cooking is complete, open hood, remove the chicken thighs to a platter and serve with additional piri-piri sauce, if desired.

Potato Cheese Crusted Chicken

SERVES: 4

PREP: 15 minutes
PREHEAT: approx. 8-10 minutes
TOTAL COOK TIME: 10 minutes

¼ cup buttermilk
1 large egg, beaten
1 cup instant potato flakes
¼ cup grated Parmesan cheese
1 tsp. salt
½ tsp. freshly ground black pepper
2 whole boneless, skinless chicken breasts (about 1 pound / 454 g each), halved
Cooking spray

1. In a shallow bowl, whisk the buttermilk and egg until blended. In another shallow bowl, stir together the potato flakes, cheese, salt, and pepper.
2. One at a time, dip the chicken pieces in the buttermilk mixture and the potato flake mixture, coating thoroughly.
3. To install the grill grate, position it flat on top of the heating element and gently press down until it sits into place. Place Air Crisp Basket on grill grate, then close the hood.
4. While holding the smoke box lid open, use the pellet scoop to pour pellets into the smoke box until filled to the top. Then close the smoke box lid.
5. Turn dial to AIR CRISP. Press WOODFIRE FLAVOR. Set temperature to 390°F, and set time to 10 minutes. Select START/STOP to begin preheating (preheating will take approx. 8–10 minutes).
6. When unit beeps to signify it has preheated and ADD FOOD is displayed, open hood and place the chicken in basket. Close hood to begin cooking.
7. With 5 minutes remaining, open hood and use silicone-tipped tongs to flip the chicken.
8. When cooking is complete, open hood, remove the chicken from basket. Let cool slightly before serving.

Mayonnaise-Mustard Chicken

SERVES: 4

PREP: 10 minutes
PREHEAT: approx. 15-19 minutes
TOTAL COOK TIME: 6 minutes

6 tbsps. mayonnaise
2 tbsps. coarse-ground mustard
2 tsps. curry powder
1 tsp. kosher salt
1 tsp. cayenne pepper
1 pound (454 g) chicken tenders

1. In a large bowl, whisk together the mayonnaise, mustard, curry powder, salt, and cayenne. Transfer half of the mixture to a serving bowl to serve as a dipping sauce. Add the chicken tenders to the large bowl and toss until well coated.
2. To install the grill grate, position it flat on top of the heating element and gently press down until it sits into place, then close the hood.
3. While holding the smoke box lid open, use the pellet scoop to pour pellets into the smoke box until filled to the top. Then close the smoke box lid.
4. Turn dial to GRILL. Press WOODFIRE FLAVOR. Set temperature to HI, and set time to 6 minutes. Select START/STOP to begin preheating (preheating will take approx. 15–19 minutes).
5. When unit beeps to signify it has preheated and ADD FOOD is displayed, open hood and place the tenders on grill grate, gently pressing them down to maximize grill marks. Close the hood and grill for 3 minutes. Then open hood, flip the tenders, and grill for another 3 minutes.
6. Use a meat thermometer to ensure the chicken has reached an internal temperature of 165ºF.
7. When cooking is complete, open hood, remove the tenders from grill. Serve the chicken with the dipping sauce.

Smoked Turkey Tenderloin

SERVES: 4

½ cup BBQ sauce
1 tbsp. spicy brown mustard
3 pounds turkey breast tenderloin
Salt and freshly ground black pepper, to taste
Olive oil spray

PREP: 20 minutes
TOTAL COOK TIME: 45 minutes

1. In a small bowl, combine the BBQ sauce and mustard to make a paste.
2. Season the turkey with salt and pepper. Spread the paste all over the turkey.
3. To install the grill grate, position it flat on top of the heating element and gently press down until it sits into place.
4. Place the turkey on the grill grate, then close the hood.
5. While holding the smoke box lid open, use the pellet scoop to pour pellets into the smoke box until filled to the top. Then close the smoke box lid.
6. Turn dial to SMOKER and set temperature to 350°F, and set time to 45 minutes. Select START/ STOP to begin cooking (preheating is not needed).
7. After 25 minutes, open hood and flip the turkey. Close hood to continue cooking.
8. Cooking is complete when an instant-read thermometer reads 165°F. When cooking is complete, open hood, remove the turkey from grill. Let the turkey rest for 10 minutes before slicing and serving.

Zesty Garlic Grilled Chicken

SERVES: 4

1½ tbsps. extra-virgin olive oil
3 garlic cloves, minced
¼ tsp. ground cumin
Sea salt
Freshly ground black pepper

Grated zest of 1 lime
Juice of 1 lime
4 boneless, skinless chicken
breasts

PREP: 5 minutes
PREHEAT: approx. 15-19 minutes
TOTAL COOK TIME: 13 minutes

1. In a large shallow bowl, stir together the oil, garlic, cumin, salt, pepper, zest, and lime juice. Add the chicken breasts and coat well. Cover and marinate in the refrigerator for 30 minutes.
2. To install the grill grate, position it flat on top of the heating element and gently press down until it sits into place, then close the hood.
3. While holding the smoke box lid open, use the pellet scoop to pour pellets into the smoke box until filled to the top. Then close the smoke box lid.
4. Turn dial to GRILL. Press WOODFIRE FLAVOR. Set temperature to HI, and set time to 13 minutes. Select START/STOP to begin preheating (preheating will take approx. 15–19 minutes).
5. When unit beeps to signify it has preheated and ADD FOOD is displayed, open hood and place the chicken breasts on grill grate, gently pressing them down to maximize grill marks. Close the hood and grill for 7 minutes. Then open hood, flip the chicken breasts, and grill for another 6 minutes.
6. When cooking is complete, open hood, remove the chicken breasts from grill. Place on a cutting board or platter to rest for 5 minutes. Serve.

Honey-Sriracha Grilled Chicken Thighs

SERVES: 4

PREP: 5 minutes
PREHEAT: approx. 15-19 minutes
TOTAL COOK TIME: 12 minutes

1 cup sriracha
Juice of 2 lemons
¼ cup honey
4 bone-in chicken thighs

1. Place the sriracha, lemon juice, and honey in a large resealable plastic bag or container. Add the chicken thighs and toss to coat evenly. Refrigerate for 30 minutes.
2. To install the grill grate, position it flat on top of the heating element and gently press down until it sits into place, then close the hood.
3. While holding the smoke box lid open, use the pellet scoop to pour pellets into the smoke box until filled to the top. Then close the smoke box lid.
4. Turn dial to GRILL. Press WOODFIRE FLAVOR. Set temperature to HI, and set time to 12 minutes. Select START/STOP to begin preheating (preheating will take approx. 15–19 minutes).
5. When unit beeps to signify it has preheated and ADD FOOD is displayed, open hood and place the chicken thighs on grill grate, gently pressing them down to maximize grill marks. Close hood to begin cooking.
6. Several times during cooking, open hood and use silicone-tipped tongs to flip the chicken thighs.
7. When cooking is complete, open hood, remove the chicken thighs from grill.Let rest for 5 minutes before serving.

Glazed Chicken Drumsticks

SERVES: 2

PREP: 5 minutes
PREHEAT: approx. 15-19 minutes
TOTAL COOK TIME: 14 minutes

4 chicken drumsticks
3 tbsps. soy sauce
2 tbsps. brown sugar
1 tsp. minced garlic
1 tsp. minced fresh ginger

1 tsp. toasted sesame oil
½ tsp. red pepper flakes
½ tsp. kosher salt
½ tsp. black pepper

1. Arrange the drumsticks in a baking pan.
2. In a medium bowl, stir together the soy sauce, brown sugar, garlic, ginger, sesame oil, red pepper flakes, salt, and black pepper. Pour the sauce over the drumsticks and toss to coat.
3. To install the grill grate, position it flat on top of the heating element and gently press down until it sits into place, then close the hood.
4. While holding the smoke box lid open, use the pellet scoop to pour pellets into the smoke box until filled to the top. Then close the smoke box lid.
5. Turn dial to GRILL. Press WOODFIRE FLAVOR. Set temperature to HI, and set time to 14 minutes. Select START/STOP to begin preheating (preheating will take approx. 15–19 minutes).
6. When unit beeps to signify it has preheated and ADD FOOD is displayed, open hood and place the drumsticks on grill grate, gently pressing them down to maximize grill marks. Close hood to begin cooking.
7. Several times during cooking, open hood and use silicone-tipped tongs to flip the drumsticks.
8. Use a meat thermometer to ensure the chicken has reached an internal temperature of 165ºF.
9. When cooking is complete, open hood, remove the drumsticks from grill. Serve hot.

Maple-Glazed Chicken Wings

SERVES: 4

1 cup maple syrup
⅓ cup soy sauce
¼ cup teriyaki sauce
3 garlic cloves, minced
2 tsps. garlic powder

2 tsps. onion powder
1 tsp. freshly ground black pepper
2 pounds bone-in chicken wings (drumettes and flats)

PREP: 5 minutes
PREHEAT: approx. 15-19 minutes
TOTAL COOK TIME: 14 minutes

1. In a large bowl, whisk together the maple syrup, soy sauce, teriyaki sauce, garlic, garlic powder, onion powder, and black pepper. Add the wings, and use tongs to toss and coat.
2. To install the grill grate, position it flat on top of the heating element and gently press down until it sits into place, then close the hood.
3. While holding the smoke box lid open, use the pellet scoop to pour pellets into the smoke box until filled to the top. Then close the smoke box lid.
4. Turn dial to GRILL. Press WOODFIRE FLAVOR. Set temperature to HI, and set time to 14 minutes. Select START/STOP to begin preheating (preheating will take approx. 15–19 minutes).
5. When unit beeps to signify it has preheated and ADD FOOD is displayed, open hood and place the chicken wings on grill grate, gently pressing them down to maximize grill marks. Close hood to begin cooking.
6. Several times during cooking, open hood and use silicone-tipped tongs to flip the wings.
7. Use a meat thermometer to ensure the chicken has reached an internal temperature of 165°F.
8. When cooking is complete, open hood, remove the chicken wings from grill. Serve hot.

Grilled Turkey Burger

SERVES: 4

1 pound ground turkey
½ red onion, minced
1 jalapeño pepper, seeded, stemmed, and minced
3 tbsps. bread crumbs
1½ tsps. ground cumin
1 tsp. paprika
½ tsp. cayenne pepper

½ tsp. sea salt
½ tsp. freshly ground black pepper
4 burger buns, for serving
Lettuce, tomato, and cheese, if desired, for serving
Ketchup and mustard, if desired, for serving

PREP: 5 minutes
PREHEAT: approx. 15-19 minutes
TOTAL COOK TIME: 10 minutes

1. In a large bowl, use your hands to combine the ground turkey, red onion, jalapeño pepper, bread crumbs, cumin, paprika, cayenne pepper, salt, and black pepper. Mix until just combined; be careful not to overwork the burger mixture.
2. Dampen your hands with cool water and form the turkey mixture into four patties.
3. To install the grill grate, position it flat on top of the heating element and gently press down until it sits into place, then close the hood.
4. While holding the smoke box lid open, use the pellet scoop to pour pellets into the smoke box until filled to the top. Then close the smoke box lid.
5. Turn dial to GRILL. Press WOODFIRE FLAVOR. Set temperature to HI, and set time to 10 minutes. Select START/STOP to begin preheating (preheating will take approx. 15–19 minutes).
6. When unit beeps to signify it has preheated and ADD FOOD is displayed, open hood and place patties on grill grate, gently pressing them down to maximize grill marks. Close the hood and grill for 5 minutes. Then open hood, flip patties, and grill for another 5 minutes.
7. Cooking is complete when the internal temperature reaches at least 165°F on a food thermometer.
8. When cooking is complete, open hood, remove patties from grill. Place each patty on a bun. Top with your preferred fixings, such as lettuce, tomato, cheese, ketchup, and/or mustard.

Greek Chicken and Veggie Kebabs

SERVES: 4

PREP: 15 minutes
PREHEAT: approx. 15-19 minutes
TOTAL COOK TIME: 12 minutes

2 tbsps. plain Greek yogurt
¼ cup extra-virgin olive oil
Juice of 4 lemons
Grated zest of 1 lemon
4 garlic cloves, minced
2 tbsps. dried oregano
1 tsp. sea salt
½ tsp. freshly ground black pepper
1 pound boneless, skinless chicken breasts, cut into 2-inch cubes
1 red onion, quartered
1 zucchini, sliced

1. In a large bowl, whisk together the Greek yogurt, oil, lemon juice, zest, garlic, oregano, salt, and pepper until well combined.
2. Place the chicken and half of the marinade into a large resealable plastic bag or container. Move the chicken around to coat evenly. Refrigerate for at least 30 minutes.
3. To install the grill grate, position it flat on top of the heating element and gently press down until it sits into place, then close the hood.
4. While holding the smoke box lid open, use the pellet scoop to pour pellets into the smoke box until filled to the top. Then close the smoke box lid.
5. Turn dial to GRILL. Press WOODFIRE FLAVOR. Set temperature to HI, and set time to 12 minutes. Select START/STOP to begin preheating (preheating will take approx. 15–19 minutes).
6. Assemble the kebabs by threading the chicken on the skewers, alternating with the red onion and zucchini. Ensure the ingredients are pushed almost completely down to the end of the skewers.
7. When unit beeps to signify it has preheated and ADD FOOD is displayed, open hood and place the kebabs on grill grate, gently pressing them down to maximize grill marks. Close the hood and grill for 6 minutes. Then open hood, flip the kebabs and coat the kebabs with the remaining marinade. Grill for another 6 minutes.
8. When cooking is complete, open hood, remove the kebabs from grill. Serve hot.

Dill Pickle Chicken Wings

SERVES: 4

PREP: 5 minutes
PREHEAT: approx. 8-10 minutes
TOTAL COOK TIME: 35 minutes

2 pounds bone-in chicken wings (drumettes and flats)
1½ cups dill pickle juice
1½ tbsps. canola oil
½ tbsp. dried dill
¾ tsp. garlic powder
Sea salt
Freshly ground black pepper

1. Place the chicken wings in a large shallow bowl. Pour the pickle juice over the top, ensuring all of the wings are coated and as submerged as possible. Cover and refrigerate for 2 hours.
2. Rinse the brined chicken wings under cool water, then pat them dry with a paper towel. Place in a large bowl.
3. In a small bowl, whisk together the oil, dill, garlic powder, salt, and pepper. Drizzle over the wings and toss to fully coat them.
4. To install the grill grate, position it flat on top of the heating element and gently press down until it sits into place. Place Air Crisp Basket on grill grate, then close the hood.
5. While holding the smoke box lid open, use the pellet scoop to pour pellets into the smoke box until filled to the top. Then close the smoke box lid.
6. Turn dial to AIR CRISP. Press WOODFIRE FLAVOR. Set temperature to 390°F, and set time to 35 minutes. Select START/STOP to begin preheating (preheating will take approx. 8–10 minutes).
7. When unit beeps to signify it has preheated and ADD FOOD is displayed, open hood and place the wings in basket. Close hood to begin cooking.
8. Several times during cooking, open hood and use silicone-tipped tongs to flip the wings.
9. Cooking is complete when the internal temperature of the chicken reaches at least 165°F on a food thermometer.
10. When cooking is complete, open hood, remove the wings from basket, and serve.

Breaded Chicken Piccata

SERVES: 2

2 large eggs
½ cup all-purpose flour
½ tsp. freshly ground black pepper
2 boneless, skinless chicken breasts

4 tbsps. unsalted butter
Juice of 1 lemon
1 tbsp. capers, drained

PREP: 5 minutes
PREHEAT: approx. 8-10 minutes
TOTAL COOK TIME: 14 minutes

1. In a medium shallow bowl, whisk the eggs until they are fully beaten.
2. In a separate medium shallow bowl, combine the flour and black pepper, using a fork to distribute the pepper evenly throughout.
3. Dredge the chicken in the flour to coat it completely, then dip it into the egg, then back in the flour.
4. To install the grill grate, position it flat on top of the heating element and gently press down until it sits into place. Place Air Crisp Basket on grill grate, then close the hood.
5. While holding the smoke box lid open, use the pellet scoop to pour pellets into the smoke box until filled to the top. Then close the smoke box lid.
6. Turn dial to AIR CRISP. Press WOODFIRE FLAVOR. Set temperature to 390°F, and set time to 10 minutes. Select START/STOP to begin preheating (preheating will take approx. 8–10 minutes).
7. When unit beeps to signify it has preheated and ADD FOOD is displayed, open hood and place the chicken breasts in basket. Close hood to begin cooking.
8. Meanwhile, melt the butter in a skillet over medium heat. Add the lemon juice and capers, and bring to a simmer. Reduce the heat to low, and simmer for 4 minutes.
9. With 5 minutes remaining, open hood and use silicone-tipped tongs to flip the chicken breasts.
10. Cooking is complete when the internal temperature of the meat reaches at least 165°F on a food thermometer.
11. When cooking is complete, open hood, remove the chicken breasts from basket. Plate the chicken, and drizzle the butter sauce over each serving.

Sweet and Spicy Turkey Meatballs

SERVES: 6

1 pound (454 g) lean ground turkey
½ cup whole-wheat panko bread crumbs
1 egg, beaten
1 tbsp. soy sauce
¼ cup plus 1 tbsp. hoisin sauce, divided

2 tsps. minced garlic
⅛ tsp. salt
⅛ tsp. freshly ground black pepper
1 tsp. sriracha
Olive oil spray

PREP: 15 minutes
PREHEAT: approx. 3 minutes
TOTAL COOK TIME: 12 minutes

1. In a large bowl, mix together the turkey, panko bread crumbs, egg, soy sauce, 1 tbsp. of hoisin sauce, garlic, salt, and black pepper.
2. Using a tablespoon, form the mixture into 24 meatballs.
3. In a small bowl, combine the remaining ¼ cup of hoisin sauce and sriracha to make a glaze and set aside.
4. To install the grill grate, position it flat on top of the heating element and gently press down until it sits into place. Place Air Crisp Basket on grill grate, then close the hood.
5. Turn dial to AIR CRISP. Set temperature to 390°F, and set time to 12 minutes. Select START/STOP to begin preheating (preheating will take approx. 3 minutes).
6. When unit beeps to signify it has preheated and ADD FOOD is displayed, open hood. Spray the basket lightly with olive oil spray and place meatballs in basket. Close hood to begin cooking.
7. After 6 minutes, open hood and brush the meatballs generously with the glaze.
8. When cooking is complete, open hood, remove the meatballs from basket, and serve hot.

Spicy Barbecue Chicken Drumsticks

SERVES: 4

PREP: 10 minutes
PREHEAT: approx. 15-19 minutes
TOTAL COOK TIME: 14 minutes

2 cups barbecue sauce
Juice of 1 lime
2 tbsps. honey
1 tbsp. hot sauce

Sea salt
Freshly ground black pepper
1 pound chicken drumsticks

1. In a large bowl, combine the barbecue sauce, lime juice, honey, and hot sauce. Season with salt and pepper. Set aside ½ cup of the sauce. Add the drumsticks to the bowl, and toss until evenly coated.
2. To install the grill grate, position it flat on top of the heating element and gently press down until it sits into place, then close the hood.
3. While holding the smoke box lid open, use the pellet scoop to pour pellets into the smoke box until filled to the top. Then close the smoke box lid.
4. Turn dial to GRILL. Press WOODFIRE FLAVOR. Set temperature to HI, and set time to 14 minutes. Select START/STOP to begin pre-heating (preheating will take approx. 15–19 minutes).
5. When unit beeps to signify it has preheated and ADD FOOD is displayed, open hood and place the drumsticks on grill grate, gently pressing them down to maximize grill marks. Close hood to begin cooking. Baste often with the sauce during cooking.
6. Cooking is complete when the internal temperature of the meat reaches at least 165°F on a food thermometer.
7. When cooking is complete, open hood, remove the drumsticks from grill. Serve hot.

Blackened Chicken Breasts

SERVES: 4

PREP: 10 minutes
PREHEAT: approx. 15-19 minutes
TOTAL COOK TIME: 13 minutes

1 large egg, beaten
¾ cup Blackened seasoning
2 whole boneless, skinless chicken breasts (about 1 pound / 454 g each), halved
Cooking spray

1. Place the beaten egg in one shallow bowl and the Blackened seasoning in another shallow bowl.
2. One at a time, dip the chicken pieces in the beaten egg and the Blackened seasoning, coating thoroughly.
3. To install the grill grate, position it flat on top of the heating element and gently press down until it sits into place, then close the hood.
4. While holding the smoke box lid open, use the pellet scoop to pour pellets into the smoke box until filled to the top. Then close the smoke box lid.
5. Turn dial to GRILL. Press WOODFIRE FLAVOR. Set temperature to HI, and set time to 13 minutes. Select START/STOP to begin pre-heating (preheating will take approx. 15–19 minutes).
6. When unit beeps to signify it has preheated and ADD FOOD is displayed, open hood and place the chicken pieces on grill grate, gently pressing them down to maximize grill marks. Close hood to begin cooking.
7. Several times during cooking, open hood and use silicone-tipped tongs to flip the chicken pieces.
8. When cooking is complete, open hood, remove the chicken pieces from grill. Let sit for 5 minutes before serving.

CHAPTER 9: SNACK AND DESSERT

Crispy Apple Chips

SERVES: 1

1 Honeycrisp or Pink Lady apple

1. Core the apple with an apple corer, leaving apple whole. Cut the apple into ⅛-inch-thick slices.
2. To install the grill grate, position it flat on top of the heating element and gently press down until it sits into place.
3. Place the apple slices in a flat single layer in the Air Crisp Basket, staggering slices as much as possible. Then place the basket on the grill grate and close the hood.
4. While holding the smoke box lid open, use the pellet scoop to pour pellets into the smoke box until filled to the top. Then close the smoke box lid.
5. Turn dial to DEHYDRATE. Press WOODFIRE FLAVOR. Set temperature to 135°F, and set time to 8 hours. Select START/STOP to begin preheating (preheating is not needed).
6. Begin to check the apple chips after 6 hours. If a crispier output is desired, continue to cook.
7. When cooking is complete, open hood and remove basket with apple chips.
8. Place the chips in a single layer on a wire rack to cool. Apples will become crisper as they cool. Serve immediately.

PREP: 5 minutes
TOTAL COOK TIME: 6-8 hours

Spiced Mixed Nuts

SERVES: 4

½ cup raw cashews
½ cup raw pecan halves
½ cup raw walnut halves
½ cup raw whole almonds
2 tbsps. olive oil
1 tbsp. light brown sugar
1 tsp. chopped fresh rosemary leaves
1 tsp. chopped fresh thyme leaves
1 tsp. kosher salt
½ tsp. ground coriander
¼ tsp. onion powder
¼ tsp. freshly ground black pepper
⅛ tsp. garlic powder

PREP: 5 minutes
PREHEAT: approx. 8-10 minutes
TOTAL COOK TIME: 6 minutes

1. In a large bowl, combine all the ingredients and toss until the nuts are evenly coated in the herbs, spices, and sugar.
2. To install the grill grate, position it flat on top of the heating element and gently press down until it sits into place. Place Air Crisp Basket on grill grate, then close the hood.
3. While holding the smoke box lid open, use the pellet scoop to pour pellets into the smoke box until filled to the top. Then close the smoke box lid.
4. Turn dial to ROAST. Press WOODFIRE FLAVOR. Set temperature to 350°F, and set time to 6 minutes. Select START/STOP to begin preheating (preheating will take approx. 8–10 minutes).
5. When unit beeps to signify it has preheated and ADD FOOD is displayed, open hood and place the nuts and seasonings in basket. Close hood to begin cooking.
6. With 5 minutes remaining, open hood and shake the basket.
7. When cooking is complete, open hood. Transfer the cocktail nuts to a bowl and serve warm.

Grilled Halloumi with Greek Salsa

SERVES: 4

PREP: 15 minutes
PREHEAT: approx. 10-12 minutes
TOTAL COOK TIME: 4 minutes

For the Salsa:
1 small shallot, finely diced
3 garlic cloves, minced
2 tbsps. fresh lemon juice
2 tbsps. extra-virgin olive oil
1 tsp. freshly cracked black pepper
½ cup finely diced English cucumber
1 plum tomato, deseeded and
  finely diced

2 tsps. chopped fresh parsley
1 tsp. snipped fresh dill
1 tsp. snipped fresh oregano
Pinch of kosher salt
For the Cheese:
1 tbsp. extra-virgin olive oil
8 ounces (227 g) Halloumi cheese,
  sliced into ½-inch-thick pieces

For the Salsa:
1. Combine the shallot, garlic, lemon juice, olive oil, pepper, and salt in a medium bowl. Add the cucumber, tomato, parsley, dill, and oregano. Toss gently to combine; set aside.

For the Cheese:
2. Place the cheese slices in a medium bowl. Drizzle with the olive oil. Toss gently to coat.
3. To install the grill grate, position it flat on top of the heating element and gently press down until it sits into place, then close the hood. Turn dial to GRILL, set temperature to HI, and set time to 4 minutes. Select START/STOP to begin cooking (preheating will take approx. 10–12 minutes).
4. When unit beeps to signify it is preheated and ADD FOOD is displayed, open hood and add the cheese slices to the grill plate. Close the hood and grill for 2 minutes. Then open hood, flip the cheese slices, and grill for another 2 minutes.
5. When cooking is complete, open hood, remove the cheese slices from grill. Divide the cheese among four serving plates. Top with the salsa and serve immediately.

Smoked Pork Ribs

SERVES: 2

PREP: 5 minutes
TOTAL COOK TIME: 2 hours

2¼ pounds (1 kg) individually cut
  St. Louis–style pork spareribs
1 tbsp. kosher salt
1 tbsp. dark brown sugar
1 tbsp. sweet paprika
1 tsp. garlic powder

1 tsp. onion powder
1 tsp. poultry seasoning
½ tsp. mustard powder
½ tsp. freshly ground black pepper

1. In a large bowl, whisk together the salt, brown sugar, paprika, garlic powder, onion powder, poultry seasoning, mustard powder, and pepper. Add the ribs and toss. Rub the seasonings into them with your hands until they're fully coated.
2. To install the grill grate, position it flat on top of the heating element and gently press down until it sits into place.
3. Place the pork on the grill grate, then close the hood.
4. While holding the smoke box lid open, use the pellet scoop to pour pellets into the smoke box until filled to the top. Then close the smoke box lid.
5. Turn dial to SMOKER and set temperature to 300°F, and set time to 2 hours. Select START/ STOP to begin cooking (preheating is not needed).
6. Flip the ribs over halfway through cooking. Cooking is complete when an instant-read thermometer reads 165°F.
7. When cooking is complete, open hood, remove the pork from grill, and let rest for 30 minutes. Serve.

Beef and Mango Skewers

SERVES: 4

1 tbsp. olive oil
¾ pound (340 g) beef sirloin tip, cut into 1-inch cubes
2 tbsps. balsamic vinegar
1 tbsp. honey

½ tsp. dried marjoram
Pinch of salt
Freshly ground black pepper, to taste
1 mango

PREP: 10 minutes
PREHEAT: approx. 15-19 minutes
TOTAL COOK TIME: 8 minutes

1. Put the beef cubes in a medium bowl and add the balsamic vinegar, olive oil, honey, marjoram, salt, and pepper. Mix well, then massage the marinade into the beef with your hands. Set aside.
2. To prepare the mango, stand it on end and cut the skin off, using a sharp knife. Then carefully cut around the oval pit to remove the flesh. Cut the mango into 1-inch cubes.
3. Thread metal skewers alternating with three beef cubes and two mango cubes.
4. To install the grill grate, position it flat on top of the heating element and gently press down until it sits into place, then close the hood.
5. While holding the smoke box lid open, use the pellet scoop to pour pellets into the smoke box until filled to the top. Then close the smoke box lid.
6. Turn dial to GRILL. Press WOODFIRE FLAVOR. Set temperature to MED, and set time to 8 minutes. Select START/STOP to begin preheating (preheating will take approx. 15–19 minutes).
7. When unit beeps to signify it is preheated and ADD FOOD is displayed, open hood and place the skewers to the grill plate. Close the hood and grill for 4 minutes. Then open hood, flip the skewers, and grill for another 4 minutes.
8. When cooking is complete, open hood, remove the skewers from grill. Serve hot.

Lemony Pear Chips

SERVES: 4

2 firm Bosc pears, cut crosswise into ⅛-inch-thick slices
1 tbsp. freshly squeezed lemon juice
½ tsp. ground cinnamon
⅛ tsp. ground cardamom

PREP: 15 minutes
TOTAL COOK TIME: 6-8 hours

1. Separate the smaller stem-end pear rounds from the larger rounds with seeds. Remove the core and seeds from the larger slices. Sprinkle all slices with lemon juice, cinnamon, and cardamom.
2. To install the grill grate, position it flat on top of the heating element and gently press down until it sits into place.
3. Place the chips in a flat single layer in the Air Crisp Basket. Then place the basket on the grill grate and close the hood.
4. While holding the smoke box lid open, use the pellet scoop to pour pellets into the smoke box until filled to the top. Then close the smoke box lid.
5. Turn dial to DEHYDRATE. Press WOODFIRE FLAVOR. Set temperature to 135°F, and set time to 8 hours. Select START/STOP to begin preheating (preheating is not needed).
6. Begin to check the chips after 6 hours. If a crispier output is desired, continue to cook.
7. When cooking is complete, open hood and remove basket with chips. Cool and serve or store in an airtight container at room temperature up for to 2 days.

Shishito Peppers with Herb Dressing

SERVES: 2

PREP: 10 minutes
PREHEAT: approx. 15-19 minutes
TOTAL COOK TIME: 6 minutes

6 ounces (170 g) shishito peppers
1 tbsp. vegetable oil
Kosher salt and freshly ground black pepper, to taste
½ cup mayonnaise
2 tbsps. finely chopped fresh basil leaves
2 tbsps. finely chopped fresh

flat-leaf parsley
1 tbsp. finely chopped fresh tarragon
1 tbsp. finely chopped fresh chives
Finely grated zest of ½ lemon
1 tbsp. fresh lemon juice
Flaky sea salt, for serving

1. In a bowl, toss together the shishitos and oil to evenly coat and season with kosher salt and black pepper.
2. To install the grill grate, position it flat on top of the heating element and gently press down until it sits into place, then close the hood.
3. While holding the smoke box lid open, use the pellet scoop to pour pellets into the smoke box until filled to the top. Then close the smoke box lid.
4. Turn dial to GRILL. Press WOODFIRE FLAVOR. Set temperature to HI, and set time to 6 minutes. Select START/STOP to begin preheating (preheating will take approx. 15–19 minutes).
5. When unit beeps to signify it is preheated and ADD FOOD is displayed, open hood and add the shishitos to the grill plate. Close the hood and grill for 3 minutes. Then open hood, flip the shishitos, and grill for another 3 minutes.
6. Meanwhile, in a small bowl, whisk together the mayonnaise, basil, parsley, tarragon, chives, lemon zest, and lemon juice.
7. When cooking is complete, open hood. Transfer the peppers to a plate, sprinkle with flaky sea salt, and serve hot with the dressing.

Rosemary-Garlic Shoestring Fries

SERVES: 2

PREP: 5 minutes
PREHEAT: approx. 8-10 minutes
TOTAL COOK TIME: 20 minutes

1 large russet potato (about 12 ounces / 340 g), scrubbed clean, and julienned
1 tbsp. olive oil
Leaves from 1 sprig fresh rosemary

1 garlic clove, thinly sliced
Kosher salt and freshly ground black pepper, to taste
Flaky sea salt, for serving

1. Place the julienned potatoes in a large colander and rinse under cold running water until the water runs clear. Spread the potatoes out on a double-thick layer of paper towels and pat dry.
2. In a large bowl, combine the potatoes, oil, and rosemary. Season with kosher salt and pepper and toss to coat evenly.
3. To install the grill grate, position it flat on top of the heating element and gently press down until it sits into place. Place Air Crisp Basket on grill grate, then close the hood.
4. While holding the smoke box lid open, use the pellet scoop to pour pellets into the smoke box until filled to the top. Then close the smoke box lid.
5. Turn dial to AIR CRISP. Press WOODFIRE FLAVOR. Set temperature to 390°F, and set time to 20 minutes. Select START/STOP to begin preheating (preheating will take approx. 8–10 minutes).
6. When unit beeps to signify it has preheated and ADD FOOD is displayed, open hood and place potatoes in basket. Close hood to begin cooking, shaking frequently during cooking.
7. With 5 minutes remaining, add the garlic and continue cooking.
8. When cooking is complete, open hood. Transfer the fries to a plate and sprinkle with flaky sea salt while they're hot. Serve immediately.

Avocado Walnut Bread

SERVES: 6

2 tbsps. olive oil
¾ cup (3 oz.) almond flour, white
2 ripe avocados, cored, peeled
  and mashed
2 large eggs, beaten
½ cup granulated swerve

¼ tsp. baking soda
2 tbsps. (¾ oz.) Toasted walnuts,
  chopped roughly
1 tsp. cinnamon ground
½ tsp. kosher salt
1 tsp. vanilla extract

PREP: 5 minutes
PREHEAT: approx. 3 minutes
TOTAL COOK TIME: 35 minutes

1. Line a 6-inch baking pan with parchment paper.
2. Mix almond flour, salt, baking soda, and cinnamon in a bowl.
3. Whisk eggs with avocado mash, yogurt, swerve, oil, and vanilla in another bowl.
4. Stir in the almond flour mixture and mix until well combined.
5. Pour the batter evenly into the pan and top with the walnuts.
6. To install the grill grate, position it flat on top of the heating element and gently press down until it sits into place, then close the hood. Turn dial to BAKE, set temperature to 310°F, set time to 35 minutes. Select START/STOP to begin preheating (preheating will take approx. 3 minutes).
7. When unit beeps to signify it is preheated and ADD FOOD is displayed, open hood and place baking pan on grill grate. Close hood to begin cooking.
8. When cooking is complete, open hood and carefully remove the bread. Cut the bread into slices to serve.

Luscious Cheesecake

SERVES: 8

3 eggs
17.6-ounce ricotta cheese
¾ cup sugar
3 tbsps. corn starch
1 tbsp. fresh lemon juice
2 tsps. vanilla extract
1 tsp. fresh lemon zest, grated finely

PREP: 10 minutes
PREHEAT: approx. 3 minutes
TOTAL COOK TIME: 25 minutes

1. Grease a baking dish lightly.
2. Mix all the ingredients in a bowl and transfer the mixture into the baking dish.
3. To install the grill grate, position it flat on top of the heating element and gently press down until it sits into place, then close the hood. Turn dial to BAKE, set temperature to 320°F, set time to 25 minutes. Select START/STOP to begin preheating (preheating will take approx. 3 minutes).
4. When unit beeps to signify it is preheated and ADD FOOD is displayed, open hood and place baking dish on grill grate. Close hood to begin cooking.
5. When cooking is complete, open hood and carefully remove the cheesecake. Serve warm.

Semolina Cake

PREP: 15 minutes
PREHEAT: approx. 3 minutes
TOTAL COOK TIME: 15 minutes

2½ cups semolina
1 cup milk
1 cup Greek yogurt
2 tsps. baking powder
½ cup walnuts, chopped
½ cup vegetable oil
1 cup sugar
Pinch of salt

1. Grease a baking pan lightly.
2. Mix semolina, oil, milk, yogurt and sugar in a bowl until well combined.
3. Cover the bowl and keep aside for about 15 minutes.
4. Stir in the baking soda, baking powder and salt and fold in the walnuts. Transfer the mixture into the baking pan.
5. To install the grill grate, position it flat on top of the heating element and gently press down until it sits into place, then close the hood. Turn dial to BAKE, set temperature to 360°F, set time to 15 minutes. Select START/STOP to begin preheating (preheating will take approx. 3 minutes).
6. When unit beeps to signify it is preheated and ADD FOOD is displayed, open hood and place baking pan on grill grate. Close hood to begin cooking.
7. When cooking is complete, open hood and carefully remove the cake. Serve warm.

Crispy Banana Slices

PREP: 15 minutes
PREHEAT: approx. 3 minutes
TOTAL COOK TIME: 15 minutes

4 medium ripe bananas, peeled and cut in 4 pieces lengthwise
⅓ cup rice flour, divided
4 tbsps. corn flour
2 tbsps. desiccated coconut
½ tsp. baking powder
½ tsp. ground cardamom
A pinch of salt

1. Mix coconut, 2 tbsps. of rice flour, corn flour, baking powder, cardamom, and salt in a shallow bowl.
2. Stir in the water gradually and mix until a smooth mixture is formed.
3. Place the remaining rice flour in a second bowl and dip the banana slices in the coconut mixture. Then dredge in the rice flour.
4. To install the grill grate, position it flat on top of the heating element and gently press down until it sits into place. Place Air Crisp Basket on grill grate, then close the hood.
5. Turn dial to AIR CRISP. Set temperature to 390°F, and set time to 15 minutes. Select START/STOP to begin preheating (preheating will take approx. 3 minutes).
6. When unit beeps to signify it has preheated and ADD FOOD is displayed, open hood and place banana slices in basket. Close hood to begin cooking.
7. Several times during cooking, open hood and use silicone-tipped tongs to flip the banana slices.
8. When cooking is complete, open hood, remove banana slices from basket, and serve hot.

Chocolate Soufflé

3 ounces semi-sweet chocolate, chopped
2 eggs, egg yolks and whites separated
¼ cup butter

3 tbsps. sugar
2 tbsps. all-purpose flour
1 tsp. powdered sugar plus extra for dusting
½ tsp. pure vanilla extract

PREP: 15 minutes
PREHEAT: approx. 3 minutes
TOTAL COOK TIME: 16 minutes

1. Grease 2 ramekins lightly.
2. Microwave butter and chocolate on high heat for about 2 minutes until smooth.
3. Whisk the egg yolks, sugar, and vanilla extract in a bowl.
4. Add the chocolate mixture and flour and mix until well combined.
5. Whisk the egg whites in another bowl until soft peaks form and fold into the chocolate mixture.
6. Sprinkle each with a pinch of sugar and transfer the mixture into the ramekins.
7. To install the grill grate, position it flat on top of the heating element and gently press down until it sits into place, then close the hood. Turn dial to BAKE, set temperature to 330°F, set time to 14 minutes. Select START/STOP to begin preheating (preheating will take approx. 3 minutes).
8. When unit beeps to signify it is preheated and ADD FOOD is displayed, open hood and place ramekins on grill grate. Close hood to begin cooking.
9. When cooking is complete, open hood and carefully remove the ramekins. Serve sprinkled with the powdered sugar to serve.

Pumpkin Bars

1 cup canned sugar free pumpkin puree
¼ cup almond butter
½ cup coconut flour
½ cup dark sugar free chocolate chips, divided
¼ cup swerve
1 tbsp. unsweetened almond milk

¾ tsp. baking soda
1 tsp. cinnamon
1 tsp. vanilla extract
¼ tsp. nutmeg
½ tsp. ginger
⅛ tsp. salt
⅛ tsp. ground cloves

PREP: 10 minutes
PREHEAT: approx. 3 minutes
TOTAL COOK TIME: 25 minutes

1. Layer a baking pan with wax paper.
2. Mix pumpkin puree, swerve, vanilla extract, milk, and butter in a bowl.
3. Combine coconut flour, spices, salt, and baking soda in another bowl.
4. Combine the two mixtures and mix well until smooth.
5. Add about ⅓ cup of the sugar free chocolate chips and transfer this mixture into the baking pan.
6. To install the grill grate, position it flat on top of the heating element and gently press down until it sits into place, then close the hood. Turn dial to BAKE, set temperature to 360°F, set time to 25 minutes. Select START/STOP to begin preheating (preheating will take approx. 3 minutes).
7. When unit beeps to signify it is preheated and ADD FOOD is displayed, open hood and place baking pan on grill grate. Close hood to begin cooking.
8. When cooking is complete, open hood and carefully remove the baked bread. Microwave the remaining sugar free chocolate bits on low heat. Top the bread with melted chocolate and slice to serve.

Flavor-Packed Clafoutis

SERVES: 4

PREP: 10 minutes
PREHEAT: approx. 3 minutes
TOTAL COOK TIME: 25 minutes

1½ cups fresh cherries, pitted
1 egg
½ cup sour cream
¼ cup flour
¼ cup powdered sugar

1 tbsp. butter
3 tbsps. vodka
2 tbsps. sugar
Pinch of salt

1. Grease a baking pan lightly.
2. Mix cherries and vodka in a bowl.
3. Sift together flour, sugar and salt in another bowl. Stir in the sour cream and egg until a smooth dough is formed.
4. Transfer the dough evenly into the baking pan and top with the cherry mixture and butter.
5. To install the grill grate, position it flat on top of the heating element and gently press down until it sits into place, then close the hood. Turn dial to BAKE, set temperature to 355°F, set time to 25 minutes. Select START/STOP to begin preheating (preheating will take approx. 3 minutes).
6. When unit beeps to signify it is preheated and ADD FOOD is displayed, open hood and place baking pan on grill grate. Close hood to begin cooking.
7. When cooking is complete, open hood and carefully remove the baking pan. Dust with powdered sugar and serve warm.

Grilled Pound Cake with Fresh Mint and Berries

SERVES: 6

PREP: 10 minutes
PREHEAT: approx. 10-12 minutes
TOTAL COOK TIME: 6 minutes

1 cup fresh raspberries
1 cup fresh blueberries
6 slices pound cake, sliced about 1-inch thick
3 tbsps. unsalted butter, at room temperature
3 tbsps. sugar
½ tbsp. fresh mint, minced

1. Evenly spread the butter on both sides of each slice of pound cake.
2. To install the grill grate, position it flat on top of the heating element and gently press down until it sits into place, then close the hood. Turn dial to GRILL, set temperature to HI, and set time to 6 minutes. Select START/STOP to begin cooking (preheating will take approx. 10–12 minutes).
3. When unit beeps to signify it is preheated and ADD FOOD is displayed, open hood and add the cake slices to the grill plate. Close the hood and grill for 3 minutes. Then open hood, flip cake slices, and grill for another 3 minutes.
4. While the cake slices cook, in a medium mixing bowl, combine the raspberries, blueberries, sugar, and mint.
5. When cooking is complete, open hood, remove cake slices from grill. Serve topped with the berry mixture.

APPENDIX 1: BASIC KITCHEN CONVERSIONS & EQUIVALENTS

DRY MEASUREMENTS CONVERSION CHART

3 teaspoons = 1 tablespoon = 1/16 cup
6 teaspoons = 2 tablespoons = 1/8 cup
12 teaspoons = 4 tablespoons = ¼ cup
24 teaspoons = 8 tablespoons = ½ cup
36 teaspoons = 12 tablespoons = ¾ cup
48 teaspoons = 16 tablespoons = 1 cup

METRIC TO US COOKING CONVERSIONS

OVEN TEMPERATURES
120 ºC = 250 ºF
160 ºC = 320 ºF
180 ºC = 350 ºF
205 ºC = 400 ºF
220 ºC = 425 ºF

LIQUID MEASUREMENTS CONVERSION CHART
8 fluid ounces = 1 cup = ½ pint = ¼ quart
16 fluid ounces = 2 cups = 1 pint = ½ quart
32 fluid ounces = 4 cups = 2 pints = 1 quart = ¼ gallon
128 fluid ounces = 16 cups = 8 pints = 4 quarts = 1 gallon

BAKING IN GRAMS
1 cup flour = 140 grams
1 cup sugar = 150 grams
1 cup powdered sugar = 160 grams
1 cup heavy cream = 235 grams

VOLUME
1 milliliter = 1/5 teaspoon
5 ml = 1 teaspoon
15 ml = 1 tablespoon
240 ml = 1 cup or 8 fluid ounces
1 liter = 34 fluid ounces

WEIGHT
1 gram = .035 ounces
100 grams = 3.5 ounces
500 grams = 1.1 pounds
1 kilogram = 35 ounces

US TO METRIC COOKING CONVERSIONS

1/5 tsp = 1 ml
1 tsp = 5 ml
1 tbsp = 15 ml
1 fluid ounces = 30 ml
1 cup = 237 ml
1 pint (2 cups) = 473 ml
1 quart (4 cups) = .95 liter
1 gallon (16 cups) = 3.8 liters
1 oz = 28 grams
1 pound = 454 grams

BUTTER
1 cup butter = 2 sticks = 8 ounces = 230 grams = 16 tablespoons

WHAT DOES 1 CUP EQUAL
1 cup = 8 fluid ounces
1 cup = 16 tablespoons
1 cup = 48 teaspoons
1 cup = ½ pint
1 cup = ¼ quart
1 cup = 1/16 gallon
1 cup = 240 ml

BAKING PAN CONVERSIONS
9-inch round cake pan = 12 cups
10-inch tube pan =16 cups
10-inch bundt pan = 12 cups
9-inch springform pan = 10 cups
9 x 5 inch loaf pan = 8 cups
9-inch square pan = 8 cups

BAKING PAN CONVERSIONS
1 cup all-purpose flour = 4.5 oz
1 cup rolled oats = 3 oz
1 large egg = 1.7 oz
1 cup butter = 8 oz
1 cup milk = 8 oz
1 cup heavy cream = 8.4 oz
1 cup granulated sugar = 7.1 oz
1 cup packed brown sugar = 7.75 oz
1 cup vegetable oil = 7.7 oz
1 cup unsifted powdered sugar = 4.4 oz

APPENDIX 2: NINJA WOODFIRE OUTDOOR GRILL TIMETABLE

BBQ SMOKER CHART

FOOD	VOLUME	PREP	TEMP	TIME	INTR TEMP
BEEF					
Chuck Roast	3-4 lbs	Season as desired	250°F	4-5 hrs	203°F
Brisket	5-9 lbs, point cut	Season as desired	250°F	5-8 hrs	206°F
Bone-In Short Ribs	6-9 pieces, 6-8 ounces each	Season as desired	275°F	4-5 hrs	203°F
Boneless Short Ribs	6-9 pieces, 6-8 ounces each	Season as desired	275°F	3-4 hrs	203°F
Tri Tip	2-3 lbs	Season as desired	325°F	20-30 mins	120°F
PORK					
Shoulder	4-5 lbs	Season as desired	250°F	4-6 hrs	203°F
Tenderloin	2-3 tenderloins, 1-2 lbs each	Season as desired	300°F	35-45 mins	145°F
Loin	3-4 lbs	Season as desired	250°F	3-4 hrs	180°-190°F
Ribs - Baby Back	1 rack, cut in half	Season as desired	300°F	1-2 hrs	190°-203°F
	2 racks, cut in half	Season as desired	300°F	1½-2 hrs	190°-203°F
Ribs - St. Louis Style	1 rack, cut in half	Season as desired	300°F	2-4 hrs	165°F
POULTRY					
Whole Chicken	4-6 lbs	Season as desired	375°F	45 mins-1½ hrs	165°F
Boneless/Bone-In Chicken Thighs	6-8 pieces, 4-6 ounces each	Season as desired	375°F	15-20 mins	165°F
Turkey Breast	3-4 lbs	Season as desired	350°F	45 mins-1½ hrs	165°F
Turkey Legs	6 pieces, 6-8 ounces each	Season as desired	375°F	30-45 mins	165°F
Duck Breast	4-6 pieces, 4-6 ounces each	Season as desired	350°F	45-60 mins	150°F
Duck Legs	4-6 pieces, 4-6 ounces each	Season as desired	350°F	45-60 mins	165°F
LAMB/VEAL					
Lamb Shanks	3-5 lbs, 1½ lbs each	Season as desired	250°F	3-5 hrs	203°F
Boneless Lamb Leg	3-6 lbs, trimmed and bound	Season as desired	250°F	6-8 hrs	203°F
Veal Shanks	3-5 lbs, 1½ lbs each	Season as desired	250°F	4-5 hrs	203°F

GRILL CHART

FOOD	VOLUME	PREP	TEMP	TIME
POULTRY				
Chicken breast, boneless	6 breasts (7-9 oz each)	season as desired	HI	13-15 mins
Chicken breast, bone-in	4 breasts (12-24 oz each)	season as desired	HI	20-25 mins
Chicken, leg quarters	3 bone-in leg quarters	season as desired	HI	15-20 mins
Chicken sausages, prepared	2 packs (8 sausages)	season as desired	HI	5-7 mins
Chicken tenderloins	9 tenderloins	season as desired	HI	6-8 mins
Chicken thighs, boneless	2 lbs	season as desired	HI	7-10 mins
Chicken thighs, bone-in	8 thighs (4-7 oz each)	season as desired	HI	12-16 mins
Chicken wings	2½ lbs	season as desired	HI	10-15 mins
Turkey burgers	6 patties	Season with salt and pepper	HI	8-11 mins
BEEF				
Beef burgers	6 patties, 1-inch thick	Season with salt and pepper	HI	5-8 mins
Filet mignon	6 steaks (6-8 oz each), 1¼-1½-inch thick	season as desired	HI	15-20 mins
Flat iron or Flank steak	1 steak (18-24 oz each) 1¼-inch thick	season as desired	HI	10-25 mins
Hot dogs	12 each	N/A	HI	5-8 mins

New York strip	4 steaks (10-12 oz each) 1¼-1½-inch thick	season as desired	HI	8-16 mins
Ribeye	3 steaks (14-16 oz each) 1¼-inch thick	season as desired	HI	10-15 mins
Skirt steak	4 steaks (10-12 oz each) 3/4-1-inch thick	season as desired	MED	7-13 mins
Steak tips	2 lbs	season as desired	MED	8-13 mins
PORK				
Baby back ribs	1 rack, divided in half	season as desired	HI	1 hr+
Bacon	6 strips, thick cut	N/A	LO	6-10 mins
Lamb rack	1 full rack (8 bones)	N/A	HI	15-20 mins
Pork chops, boneless	6-8 boneless chops (8 oz each)	season as desired	HI	10-14 mins
Pork chops, bone-in	4 thick cut, bone-in (10-12 oz each)	season as desired	HI	15-18 mins
Pork tenderloins	3 whole tenderloins (1-1½ lbs each)	season as desired	MED	18-22 mins
Sausages	10 each	N/A	LO	8-12 mins
SEAFOOD				
Flounder	3 fillets	Coat with oil, season as desired	HI	4-6 mins
Halibut	6 fillets (5-6 oz each)	Coat with oil, season as desired	HI	6-10 mins
Salmon	6 fillets (6 oz each)	Coat with oil, season as desired	HI	7-11 mins
Scallops	18 each	Coat with oil, season as desired	HI	4-6 mins
Shrimp (large or jumbo)	1½ lbs	Coat with oil, season as desired	HI	4-5 mins
Swordfish	2 steaks (11-12 oz each)	Coat with oil, season as desired	HI	8-10 mins
Tuna	4 steaks (4-6 oz each)	Coat with oil, season as desired	HI	6-10 mins

GRILL CHART

FOOD	VOLUME	PREP	TEMP	TIME
VEGGIES				
Asparagus	2 bunches	Trimmed, coat with oil, season as desired	HI	8-12 mins
Baby Bok Choy	1½ lbs	Coat with oil, season as desired	HI	9-13 mins
Bell Peppers	4	Cut into quarters, coat with oil, season as desired	HI	6-12 mins
Broccoli	2 heads	Cut into 1-inch pieces, coat with oil, season as desired	HI	10-16 mins
Brussel Sprouts	2 lbs	Halved, trimmed, coat with oil, season as desired	HI	11-16 mins
Carrots	2 lbs	Peel, cut into 1 or 2-inch pieces, coat with oil, season as desired	HI	20-23 mins
Cauliflower	2 heads	Cut into 1-inch pieces, coat with oil, season as desired	HI	20-24 mins
Corn on the cob	4 cobs	Coat with oil, season as desired	HI	10-15 mins
Crimini mushrooms	2 lbs	Clean, coat with oil, season as desired	HI	6-9 mins
Eggplant	2 medium	Sliced, coat with oil, season as desired	HI	7-10 mins
Green beans	24 oz	Trimmed, coat with oil, season as desired	HI	12-20 mins
Onions, white or red (cut in half)	6	Peeled, cut in half, coat with oil, season as desired	HI	8-12 mins
Onions, white or red (sliced)	3	Peeled, sliced, coat with oil, season as desired	HI	6-10 mins
Portobello mushrooms	6	Cleaned, coat with oil, season as desired	HI	7-9 mins
Squash or zucchini	1 lb	Cut in quarters lengthwise, coat with oil, season as desired	HI	6-10 mins
Tomatoes	6	Cut in half, coat with oil, season as desired	HI	6-10 mins
FRUIT				
Avocado	6-8	Cut in half, remove pits, spray grill with nonstick cooking spray	HI	3-5 mins
Bananas	4	Peel, cut in half lengthwise	HI	4 mins
Lemons & limes	5	Cut in half lengthwise	HI	4 mins
Mango	4-6	Cut in half, remove skins and pits	HI	4-8 mins
Melon	6-8 spears	N/A	HI	4-6 mins
Pineapple	6-8 slices or spears	Cut in 2-inch pieces	HI	5-8 mins

Stone Fruit	6-8	Cut in half, remove pits, press cut-side down	HI	5-7 mins
		BREAD/CHEESE		
Bread (baguette or ciabatta)	12-16-inch loaf	Cut in 1½-inch slices, brushed with oil	HI	3-5 mins
Halloumi Cheese	24-36 oz	Cut in ½-inch slices	HI	3-6 mins

FROZEN GRILL CHART

FOOD	VOLUME	PREP	TEMP	TIME
		FROZEN POULTRY		
Chicken breast, boneless	6 breasts (7-9 oz each)	season as desired	MED	18-22 mins
Chicken thighs, bone-in	6 thighs (4-7 oz each)	season as desired	MED	20-25 mins
Turkey burgers	4-6 patties	Season with salt and pepper	MED	6-10 mins
		FROZEN BEEF		
Beef burgers	6 patties, 1-inch thick	Season with salt and pepper	MED	7-12 mins
Filet Mignon	6 steaks (6-8 oz each) 1¼-1½-inch thick	season as desired	MED	17-22 mins
New York strip	4 steaks (10-12 oz each) 1¼-1½-inch thick	season as desired	MED	17-21 mins
Ribeye	3 steaks (14-16 oz each) 1¼-inch thick	season as desired	MED	20-25 mins
		FROZEN PORK		
Pork chops, boneless	6-8 boneless chops (8 oz each)	season as desired	MED	15-20 mins
Pork chops, bone-in	4 thick cut, bone-in (10-12 oz each)	season as desired	HI (375°F)	23-27 mins
Pork tenderloins	2 whole tenderloins (1-1½ lbs each)	season as desired	MED	17-23 mins
Sausages, uncooked	10-12 each	N/A	LO	12-18 mins
		FROZEN SEAFOOD		
Halibut	6 fillets (5-6 oz each)	Coat with oil, season as desired	HI	13-17 mins
Salmon	6 fillets (6 oz each)	Coat with oil, season as desired	HI	13-17 mins
Shrimp (large or jumbo)	1½ lbs	Coat with oil, season as desired	HI	5-6 mins
		FROZEN VEGETARIAN		
Veggie burger	6 patties	N/A	HI	8-10 mins

AIR CRISP CHART

FOOD	VOLUME	PREP	TEMP	TIME
		FROZEN FOODS		
Chicken cutlets	6 cutlets	N/A	390°F	15-18 mins
Chicken nuggets	2-3 boxes (24-36 oz)	N/A	390°F	13-15 mins
Fish fillets	12 fillets, breaded	N/A	390°F	10-15 mins
Fish sticks	30 fish sticks (22 oz, approx. 2 boxes)	N/A	390°F	10-13 mins
French fries	1 lb	N/A	350°F	18-20 mins
French fries	2 lbs	N/A	350°F	23-27 mins
French fries	4 lbs	N/A	390°F	30-40 mins
Mozzarella sticks	1 large box (32 oz)	N/A	375°F	6-8 mins
Pot stickers	2 lbs	N/A	390°F	15-20 mins
Pizza rolls	1 large bag (approx. 100ct)	N/A	390°F	10-15 mins
Popcorn shrimp	2 boxes (24 oz)	N/A	390°F	10-13 mins
Sweet potato fries	1 bag (approx. 20-24 oz)	N/A	390°F	17-21 mins
Sweet potato fries	2 bags (approx. 40 oz)	N/A	390°F	20-25 mins
Tater tots	1 bag (approx. 24 oz)	N/A	390°F	15-18 mins
		PORK		
Pork chops, boneless	6-8 boneless chops (8 oz each)	seasoned as desired	390°F	20-23 mins
Pork chops, bone-in	4 thick cut, bone-in (10-12 oz each)	seasoned as desired	390°F	20-23 mins
Pork tenderloins	3 whole tenderloins (1-1½ lbs each)	seasoned as desired	390°F	20-25 mins
Bacon	6 strips, thick cut	N/A	390°F	10-13 mins
Sausages	10 each	N/A	390°F	10-13 mins

POULTRY				
Chicken breast, boneless	4-6 breasts (½-¾ lb each)	seasoned as desired	390°F	8-13 mins
Chicken thighs, boneless	2 lbs	seasoned as desired	390°F	12-17 mins
Chicken thighs, bone-in	6 (4-7 oz each)	seasoned as desired	390°F	15-20 mins
Chicken wings	3½ lbs	seasoned as desired	390°F	40-50 mins
VEGETABLES				
Asparagus	2 bunches	Trimmed, coat with oil, season as desired	390°F	6-9 mins
Beets	6	Peeled, coat with oil, season as desired	390°F	25-30 mins
Bell peppers	4-6 peppers	Cut into quarters, coat with oil, season as desired	400°F	9-13 mins
Broccoli	2 heads	Cut into 1-inch pieces, coat with oil, season as desired	390°F	10-13 mins
Brussel sprouts	2-3 lbs	Halved, trimmed, coat with oil, season as desired	390°F	20-30 mins
Carrots	2 lbs	Peeled, cut into 1 or 2-inch pieces, coat with oil, season as desired	390°F	20-23 mins
Cauliflower	2-3 heads (2-4 lbs total)	Cut into 1-inch pieces, coat with oil, season as desired	390°F	30-40 mins
Corn on the Cob	4-6 cobs	Coat with oil, season as desired	390°F	10-15 mins
Kale (for chips)	8 cups, packed	Coat with oil, season as desired	390°F	8-11 mins
Green beans	24 oz	Trimmed, coat with oil, season as desired	390°F	15-20 mins
Mushrooms	2-3 lbs	Halved or sliced, coat with oil, season as desired	390°F	7-9 mins
Potatoes, russet	3 lbs	Cut in 1-inch wedges, toss with 1-3 Tbsp oil	390°F	25-30 mins
	2 lbs	Hand-cut fries, thin, toss with 1-3 Tbsp oil	390°F	22-24 mins
	2 lbs	Hand-cut fries, thick, toss with 1-3 Tbsp oil	390°F	25-30 mins
	6-8 whole	Pierce with a fork	390°F	45-50 mins
Potatoes, sweet	2 lbs	Cut in 1-inch chunks, toss with 1-3 Tbsp oil	390°F	30-35 mins
	6-8 whole	Pierce with a fork	390°F	50-55 mins
Squash or zucchini	1 pound	Cut in quarters lengthwise, coat with oil, season as desired	390°F	10-14 mins

DEHYDRATE CHART

INGREDIENT	PREPARATION	TEMP	DEHYDRATE TIME
FRUITS & VEGETABLES			
Apples	Cut in ⅛-inch slices, remove core, rinse in lemon water, pat dry	135°F	6-8 hrs
Asparagus	Cut in 1-inch pieces, blanch	135°F	6-8 hrs
Bananas	Peel, cut in ⅜-inch slices	135°F	6-8 hrs
Beets	Peel, cut in ⅛-inch slices	135°F	6-8 hrs
Eggplant	Peel, cut in ¼-inch slices, blanch	135°F	6-8 hrs
Fresh herbs	Rinse, pat dry, remove stems	135°F	4 hrs
Ginger root	Cut in ⅜-inch slices	135°F	6 hrs
Mangoes	Peel, cut in ⅜-inch slices, remove pit	135°F	6-8 hrs
Mushrooms	Clean with soft brush (do not wash)	135°F	6-8 hrs
Pineapple	Peel, cut in ⅜-½-inch slices, remove core	135°F	6-8 hrs
Strawberries	Cut in half or in ½-inch slices	135°F	6-8 hrs
Tomatoes	Cut in ⅜-inch slices; blanch if planning to rehydrate	135°F	6-8 hrs
MEAT, POULTRY, FISH			
Beef jerky	Cut in ¼-inch slices, marinate overnight	150°F	5-7 hrs
Chicken jerky	Cut in ¼-inch slices, marinate overnight	150°F	5-7 hrs
Turkey jerky	Cut in ¼-inch slices, marinate overnight	150°F	5-7 hrs
Salmon jerky	Cut in ¼-inch slices, marinate overnight	165°F	3-5 hrs

APPENDIX 3: RECIPES INDEX

Printed in Great Britain
by Amazon

47507010R00051